CRITICAL ACCLAIM FOR HAROLD KUSHNER'S COMPELLING *NEW YORK TIMES* BESTSELLER

WHO NEEDS GOD

"In *WHO NEEDS GOD,* Kushner glides thoughtfully and literately from Elie Wiesel to William James to African mythology to make his case for God's role in our lives. The most compelling argument, not surprisingly, is . . . that only religion provides answers that enable people to confront their mortality."

—*Newsweek*

"Here's a book about God and faith that is, surprisingly, ideal for the reader who has rejected religion."

—Joyce Maynard, *Mademoiselle*

"Kushner remains superbly rational . . . likable and persuasive. . . . No mystical tangents here, either traditional or New Age."

—*The Sun* (Baltimore)

"There is a note of awe and humility in nearly all of his counseling, which has become a Kushner trademark. Listening rather than speaking in times of crisis and showing the need for morality rather than preaching about it are only two examples. . . . Kushner is an author who speaks like an old friend of the family and promises never to mislead us with facile answers that fail to satisfy."

—*Detroit Free Press*

"Kushner invites his readers to rethink the role of religion in their lives, as a way of seeing that it provides an alternative to the widespread emptiness they confront. . . . *WHO NEEDS GOD* is richly concrete and nuanced . . . sensitive and instructive."

—*The Plain Dealer* (Cleveland)

"Kushner powerfully explores the importance of God and religious faith in our daily lives. *WHO NEEDS GOD* is written for all religions—those who have either lost their faith, drifted away from organized religion, or have difficulty believing that religion can be important in the 20th century."

—*St. Louis Jewish Light*

Books by Harold Kushner

Who Needs God
When All You've Ever Wanted Isn't Enough
When Bad Things Happen to Good People
When Children Ask About God
Commanded to Live

HAROLD KUSHNER

WHO NEEDS GOD

POCKET BOOKS
New York London Toronto Sydney Singapore

Translations of the Psalms in chapters 3, 4, 6, 7, and 9 are from the *Tanakh*, a New Translation of the Holy Scriptures, by the Jewish Publication Society, Philadelphia, Pennsylvania, and used by permission of the Jewish Publication Society.

Letter in chapter 6 used by permission of Ann Landers, *The Los Angeles Times*, Creators Syndicates.

POCKET BOOKS, a division of Simon & Schuster, Inc.
1230 Avenue of the Americas, New York, NY 10020

ISBN: 0-7434-1190-0

First Pocket Books trade paperback printing December 2000

10 9 8 7 6 5 4 3 2 1

POCKET and colophon are registered trademarks of Simon & Schuster, Inc.

Cover design by Carolyn Lechter

Printed in the U.S.A.

For Suzette
"Rejoice with the wife of your youth,
a doe of love." [Proverbs 5:18]

CONTENTS

WHO
NEEDS
GOD

INTRODUCTION

I WROTE THIS BOOK BECAUSE I HAD TO. I love the religious tradition out of which I come and I love the several hundred members of the congregation I serve. The enduring frustration of my rabbinic career has been my inability to get my two loves to find and love each other.

I deal with bright, successful people, people I genuinely like and admire, and I sense that something is missing in their lives. There is a lack of rootedness, a sense of having to figure things out by themselves because the past cannot be trusted as their guide. Their celebrations, from their children's birthday parties to a daughter's wedding to a business milestone, can be lots of fun but rarely soar to the level of joy. And as they grow older, I suspect they either confront or actively hide from confronting the thought that "there must be more to life than this."

There is a spiritual vacuum at the center of their lives,

and their lives betray this lack of an organizing vision, a sense of "this is who I am and what my life is fundamentally about." Some look for that center in their work, and are disappointed when corporations choose not to repay the loyalty they demanded or when retirement leaves them feeling useless. Some try to find it in their families, and don't understand why they are so hurt when adolescent children insist, "Let me lead my own life!" and adult children move to another state and call every other Sunday. And for some reason, it never occurs to them to ask, "How did previous generations find meaning in their lives?"

For almost thirty years, I have tried to show my congregants how much more fulfilled they would be if they made room for their religious tradition in their lives. I have urged them to do it, not to make God happy but to make themselves happy. I have told them the Hassidic story of the man who got a telegram telling him that a relative had died and left him some valuable property. He was to contact the rabbi for details. Excited, he went to the rabbi, only to be told that the relative was Moses and the valuable property was the Jewish religious tradition. And much of the time, they reacted as I suspect the man in the story did, disappointed that their legacy was religious wisdom and not downtown real estate.

This book is the product of those years of thinking and teaching on the issue of what we lose when we become too intellectual or too modern to make room for religion in our lives. It is about what has happened to the souls of modern men and women under the impact of modern life, what we have lost in the process of gaining personal freedom and material comfort. But more than that, it is a summary of what my own life has been about, what has gotten me through bad times and taught me how to celebrate the good times, how I have learned to recognize the extraordinary things that even the most ordinary lives contain. In the course of the book, I will be using illustrations from the Book of Psalms, as I have used the Books of Job and Ecclesiastes in my previous writings, to ground my comments in Scriptural tradition and to show how wise and sensitive people of another time dealt with the timeless questions we face today.

The thesis of this book is that there is a kind of nourishment our souls crave, even as our bodies need the right foods, sunshine, and exercise. Without that spiritual nourishment, our souls remain stunted and undeveloped. In the physical realm, we understand that our ancestors' hard physical work built muscles and burned off calories, but we today are the victims of a modern lifestyle, so we need to diet, to jog, to work out at the gym. So, too, the kind of spiritual communion our forebears knew is less accessible to us—because the world is so noisy and full of distractions, because we are so dazzled by our power and success, because religion in the late twentieth century is often badly packaged or presented by people we cannot trust or admire.

The members of a certain West African tribe tell the legend of the Sky Maiden. It happened once that the people of the tribe noticed their cows were giving less milk than they used to. They could not understand why.

One young man volunteered to stay up all night to see what might be happening. After several hours of waiting in the darkness, hiding in a bush, he saw something extraordinary. A young woman of astonishing beauty rode a moonbeam down from heaven to earth, carrying a large pail. She milked the cows, filled her pail, and climbed back up the moonbeam to the sky. The man could not believe what he had seen. The next night, he set a trap near where the cows were kept, and when the maiden came down to milk the cows, he sprang the trap and caught her. "Who are you?" he demanded.

She explained that she was a Sky Maiden, a member of a tribe that lived in the sky and had no food of their own. It was her job to come to earth at night and find food. She pleaded with him to let her out of the net and she would do anything he asked. The man said he would release her only if she agreed to marry him. "I will marry you," she said, "but first you must let me go home for three days to prepare myself. Then I will return and be your wife." He agreed.

Three days later she returned, carrying a large box. "I will be your wife and make you very happy," she told him, "but you must promise me never to look inside this box."

For several weeks they were very happy together. Then one day, while his wife was out, the man was overcome with curiosity and opened the box. There was nothing in it. When the woman came back, she saw her husband looking strangely at her and said, "You looked in the box, didn't you? I can't live with you anymore."

"Why?" the man asked. "What's so terrible about my peeking into an empty box?"

"I'm not leaving you because you opened the box. I thought you probably would. I'm leaving you because you said it was empty. It wasn't empty; it was full of sky. It contained the light and the air and the smells of my home in the sky. When I went home for the last time, I filled that box with everything that was most precious to me to remind me of where I came from. How can I be your wife if what is most precious to me is emptiness to you?"

This book contains what is most precious to me, the ideas and the affirmations on which I have based my life, the thoughts and guidelines with which I have tried to help others bring depth and order into their lives. I hope you will not find it empty.

CHAPTER

1

DOES GOD REALLY MAKE A DIFFERENCE?

"I DON'T BELIEVE IN ORGANIZED RELIGION."
Paul was a child of the sixties, with his long hair and casual dress. It was one morning in the early 1970s that he sat opposite me in my study. He had called to ask to see me during his college vacation, more as a favor to his father, an active member of my synagogue, than out of any expectation that I would change his mind.

He told me, "I believe in God. I believe in being kind to people, treating them right, not hurting them. I believe in trying to make the world a better place. But I don't see why you need churches and synagogues, fancy buildings that are always looking for money. I don't see why you need professional clergy (nothing personal, Rabbi), prayer books, organized services, rules and rituals that nobody understands. I don't see why you need so many different religions, all arguing with each other. Why isn't it enough just to tell everybody to be nice to each other?"

He and I spoke for about an hour. I told him that

some people can create lives of holiness all by themselves, the way Mozart could create immortal music
without taking piano lessons, but that most of us need a
structure and the company of other people to do it. I
spoke to him of the need for community, that even if he
didn't need organized religion, he should feel the obligation to maintain it for the people who did. (I restrained
myself from telling him that if he didn't like organized
religion, he had come to the right place; our synagogue
was so disorganized it didn't deserve that description.) I
spoke of the time-tested wisdom of a tradition thousands of years old, and urged him to accept what it had
learned rather than dwell on its mistakes. Paul spoke of
how boring his religious education had been when he
was a child, how meaningless he found the services he
attended with his parents whenever he was home, and
how his science and psychology courses at school had
helped him to understand why people living in less
enlightened times might have needed religion, and why
we no longer need it today.

After an hour, we parted cordially. Paul went back to
school. Ultimately, he got married, got a haircut, moved
to another state, and has become moderately active in a
synagogue there, more, I suspect, as a return to his
father's example than as a result of anything I told him
that morning. I don't know if he ever thinks about the
conversation we had that day. I think of it often.

This book is written for Paul, the bright, idealistic
young man who asked why we need more than the commandment to be nice to each other. It is written for the
young woman from a religiously committed home who

went off to college and wrote a paper for her freshman English class on why religion harms more people than it helps. It is written for the man and woman from different religious backgrounds who fall in love and can't understand why religion is a source of conflict in their lives rather than a source of joy and inspiration. And it is written for all the intelligent, thoughtful people I have met in my travels—journalists, radio talk-show hosts, strangers who struck up a conversation with me on a plane—who had trouble believing that religion could be important to somebody in the twentieth century. This book is written for all the people who don't know that they are religious—good, honest, caring people who dismiss their local church or synagogue as irrelevant to their lives or find their way to it only at times of emergency or family celebration. (A neighbor once told me, "I think of your synagogue the way I think of Massachusetts General Hospital. I'm glad my life is stable enough that I don't need it often, but when I need it, I'm glad there is a good one around.") Should these same good people feel vaguely lonely, disconnected, unfulfilled, confused by the hard choices they are called on to make in today's world, they will probably never understand the connection between that vague sense of unease and the absence of religion in their lives.

Recent years have not been kind to the cause of organized religion. Prominent religious personalities have been found to be just as vulnerable to sexual and financial temptations as the rest of us. We read about the very comfortable lifestyles of leading clergymen, or of the corrupt business practices of wealthy donors whom religious organizations have seen fit to honor, and we begin to worry that the dollars in the collection plate are tainted both by the source they come from and by the uses to which they will be put. Churches and synagogues have too often been breeding grounds for hypocrisy, self-righteousness, and small-mindedness instead of being fountains of charity and piety. No wonder that religion has lost its central place in the lives of so many Americans, becoming just one more leisure-time activity, competing for whatever time and energy we have left over after we have done the "important" things in our lives, attracting mostly people who need or enjoy "that sort of thing" and dismissed casually by the rest of us. Even those people who have rediscovered religion in recent years and have given themselves totally to it have not always done much to advance its cause. Their enthusiasm often expresses itself in a fundamentalism bordering on fanaticism, a dogmatism that makes others uncomfortable, an unseemly arrogance in presuming to speak in God's name and condemning anyone who disagrees with them.

In fact, the past few centuries have not been kind to the cause of organized religion. It may have begun with Copernicus and Galileo discovering that the earth was not the center of the universe—that the sun did not revolve around it—and that the Biblical description of the cosmos was inaccurate. Then Darwin taught that human beings evolved from more primitive animals by a blind, morally neutral process of evolution over a period of millions of years. Finally Freud came along and took away our cherished belief that our rational minds made us different from other creatures.

The nineteenth and twentieth centuries have been marked by the enthronement of Science, the objective search for truth that could be tested and verified, in place of Faith, which came more and more to be seen as fairy tales and wishful thinking. Religion, we were told, was an effort to understand and control the unknown, and as more and more became known about how the world worked, the domain of religion grew smaller and smaller.

At the end of the Book of Job, God confronts those who would challenge Him by saying, "Do you know who fixed [the earth's dimensions], or measured it with a line? . . . Do you know the seasons when the mountain goats give birth? Can you mark the time when the hinds calve?" (Job 38:5, 39:1) But modern man has found ways to measure the earth. He has studied the mating habits of the wild goat, and even intervened to keep it from becoming an endangered species. Are those grounds for being less impressed with God than our ancestors were?

To make matters worse, spokesmen for organized religion tried to challenge the scientific discoveries of Galileo, Darwin, Freud, and others, asking the faithful, "Which side are you on?" I have heard otherwise intelligent people tell me that, when God created the world six thousand years ago, along with the mountains and rivers He created *dinosaur fossils* (not dinosaurs). Why? For no reason except to test the faith of people who would one day live in a scientific age. Would they believe in revealed Scripture or in the misleading results of carbon-14 dating? To the embarrassment of those religious spokesmen (and, they would assure us, to the dismay of God as well), modern men and women have overwhelmingly chosen truth over orthodoxy, and have learned to see religion as the enemy of honesty, progress, and science.

With a bit more wisdom, might not these religious leaders have seen that same trend as a victory for the cause of religion rather than a defeat? That men and women chose to use their God-given intelligence to explore and understand God's world was a religious act. To seek to understand why earthquakes happen and what causes disease is not an arrogant encroachment on God's domain; it is an example of human beings, in God's image, extending God's process of creation by bringing order in place of chaos. To search for truth instead of relying on ancient guesswork is a religious affirmation, not a repudiation. What religion worthy of its name would base itself on the hope that people would be too intimidated to find out how the world really works? One of my favorite passages in the entire Bible is in chapter 13 of the Book of Job. Job's friends have tried to explain the disasters which have befallen him by assuring him that God knows what is right for the world better than he does, and warn that it is blasphemous for him to complain about God. Job answers them:

Will you speak unjustly on God's behalf?
Will you speak deceitfully for Him? . . .

What will happen when He examines you?
Will you fool Him as one fools men? [Job 13:7–9]

The friends have cautioned Job, "You're saying terrible things about God, and He's going to be very angry at you." Job replies, "If God is a God worth worshiping, I have to believe that He respects my honesty more than your flattery. I may be theologically wrong in what I say about God, but I am saying what I think and feel to be true, not what I think God wants to hear, and I have to believe that God respects that."

Some readers will remember that in October 1973 the Egyptian and Syrian armies attacked Israel on the morning of Yom Kippur, the Day of Atonement, when all Jews spend the day in synagogue, praying and fasting. Many lives were lost in those first hours of fighting. I heard of a man who went to his rabbi a few days later and told him: "When I heard the news about the fighting in Israel, I slammed my prayer book shut and walked out of synagogue. I said to myself, If God is going to let young Jewish boys be killed for defending their country on Yom Kippur, I'm not going to sit here reciting psalms of praise to Him. I walked out of temple and spent the rest of the day sitting at home, angry at God. Now, three days later, I feel embarrassed by what I did. I feel guilty for walking out on the Yom Kippur service, and I want to know what I can do to make up for it."

The rabbi told him, "You have nothing to feel guilty about and nothing to apologize for. Your slamming the book down and storming out was probably the most sincere prayer anybody offered in synagogue all day long. The God I believe in is not so fragile that you hurt Him by being angry at Him, or so petty that He will hold it against you for being upset with Him. I believe He is just as upset about people being killed in the war as you and I are, and He respects good, clean, honest anger as much as you and I do, and a lot more than He respects mumbled prayers by people going through the motions."

I have to admit that some of my best friends are atheists. They never darken the doorway of either church or synagogue. They don't believe in a Supreme Being. They never pray; in some cases, I'm not sure they even understand what it means to pray. And yet they are good, caring, honest people, sensitive to the needs of others, generous with their time, their love, their property. And then there are people—as a clergyman, I run into them all too often—who are always at services, always invoking the name of God in their conversations. And so often they turn out to be small-souled people, insecure and judgmental, quick to find fault with others.

To be fair, I should also say that I know many regular church- and synagogue-goers who are wonderful, warm, almost saintly people, and many nonbelievers who take their rejection of religion as a license to practice selfishness and deceit. But in a sense, that only sharpens the question: What difference does the commitment to religion make in a person's life? If religious belief and church attendance don't necessarily make you a good person, and nonattendance and rejection of religion don't necessarily make you a bad one, what is the point of being religious? What does the religious person get out of his or her faith that the nonreligious person has to do without? Is it something we would all be better off for having, or something that only some people—the weak and insecure, the spiritually inclined—need, and the rest of us can do without?

My answer to that question will be largely a personal one. I can't speak of what religion offers people in general, but I can speak of what it has come to mean to me, how it has shaped my life, and of the impact it has had on the lives of people I have known, people who turned to me as their rabbi, bringing me their problems, their pain, the shattered fragments of their broken dreams.

Paul, whose conversation with me years ago ultimately flowered into this book, assured me that while he did not believe in religion, he believed in God. I asked him what he meant by that, and he told me that when he contemplates the beauty and intricacy of the world, he has to believe that God exists. That's very nice, I told him, and I'm sure that God appreciates your vote of confidence. But for the religious mind and soul, the issue has never been the *existence* of God but the *importance* of God, the difference that God makes in the way we live. To believe that God exists the way you believe that the South Pole exists, though you have never seen either one, to believe in the reality of God the way you believe in the Pythagorean theorem, as an accurate abstract statement that does not really affect your daily life, is not a religious stance. A God who exists but does not matter, who does not make a difference in the way you live, might as well not exist. He would be like a modern European king, a benevolent figurehead trotted out for ceremonial occasions and beloved by everyone because he never does anything. The issue is not what God is like. The issue is what kind of people we become when we attach ourselves to God.

This, then, is our question: In a world where atheists are often wonderful people and ostensibly religious people disappoint us, in a world where God is a remote presence even for people who claim to believe in Him, what promise does religion hold for us? What can it offer? What difference does it really make in our lives?

CHAPTER

2

EYES WITH WHICH TO SEE THE WORLD

RELIGION IS NOT PRIMARILY A SET OF beliefs, a collection of prayers, or a series of rituals. Religion is first and foremost a way of seeing. It can't change the facts about the world we live in, but it can change the way we see those facts, and that in itself can often make a real difference.

You and I visit the same hospital. We walk down the same corridor and we see the same things—elderly patients for whom length of days has become a curse instead of a blessing; young people whose lives have been shattered by vicious criminals or drunk-driving accidents; innocent children who are victims of genetic tragedy and will never really have a chance to live. The facts are the same for each of us, but do we really see the same things? One person will see an endless chronicle of pain and suffering, and conclude that the world is a mess and life is Somebody's idea of a nasty joke. For him, it is a mistake to care too much about anything in this world; you just set yourself up to have your heart broken. (A friend of mine who used to be a nurse tells me of going into a hospital room where a teenage girl sat by the bedside of her boyfriend, who was dying of cancer, and asking, "Is there anything I can do for you?" The girl answered, "Yeah, remind me never to love anybody this much again.") Another person, seeing the same situation, will come away having learned something about human courage and resiliency. Her conclusion will be that incurable illnesses are a painful outrage *precisely because* life is good and holy. Otherwise why would it grieve us so much when a life is cut short? For her, the courage to love in the face of the world's unfairness is the most profoundly human response.

For the doctor, illness and trauma are a challenge to practice the healing skills. For the chaplain, they represent opportunities to make real the presence of God as a God who loves all of His creatures, not a God of judgment or detachment. For both these people, the facts, the medical diagnoses are the same. But the eyes with which they see those facts determine how they will act, not only within the walls of the hospital but when they leave and encounter the world outside.

In chapter 21 of the Book of Genesis, Hagar, Abraham's concubine, who had borne him a child while his wife Sarah was childless, incurs the anger and jealousy of Sarah. Hagar and her son are banished into the desert. Before long, they are lost and out of water. The child is at the point of dying of thirst. Hagar puts him down under a bush, turns away, and begins to weep. God hears her crying, and we read, "God opened her eyes and she saw a well of water, and she went and filled her bottle, and gave the boy to drink." (Genesis 21:19) God did not make a miracle happen for Hagar as we usually understand that term. He did not create any life-giving resources that were not there before. He *opened her eyes* so that she saw the well that she had not previously noticed, and all of a sudden the same world which had looked so hopelessly cruel to her a moment before was now seen as a livable and life-sustaining place. The well had been there all along. The world was never really as bleak and barren a place as it had seemed to her. But until God opened her eyes and led her to see the water, she looked at life and saw only futility and suffering.

I think of a man in my congregation whose wife left him and ran off with her lover. The rejection crushed him, leaving him feeling unlovable. He came to see me once a week for more than a month, and each time he came to my office he showed the hallmarks of serious depression. He shuffled into the room, eyes downcast, handshake limp. His voice was so low as to be barely audible, and I frequently had to ask him to repeat what he had said. No matter what I said to him, he exuded an air of despair and hopelessness. Then one evening when he showed up for his appointment, the knock on the door was loud and firm. His posture was erect, his eyes sparkled. I could have guessed what happened before he told me. He had met someone, a woman who found him attractive and compassionate, and suddenly the world looked different to him. It was the same world he had been complaining about for six weeks. Nothing had changed except the eyes through which he now saw it.

Religion has to mean more to us than a commitment to ethical behavior, to loving our neighbors. It has to teach our eyes how to see the world. I can't prove to you that a human life is special and of unique value, any more than someone else can prove to you that it isn't. I can only suggest to you that some wonderful and liberating things (and also some difficult and demanding things) happen to you when you come to see life through the eyes of religious faith. I can only suggest that there is something innate in each of us that responds to the idea that human life is sacred, an instinctive feeling that this is true. When we have learned to see life religiously, we will understand why we have certain commitments that have no basis in logic or science: that the birth of a child is something wondrous, worthy of celebration, and that the death of a child is a searing tragedy; that it makes sense to spend thousands of dollars and hundreds of man-hours to rescue one person from a collapsed building; that an elderly widow has a right to enjoy life and not be left alone to await her own death; that there is nothing we can do this afternoon more important than visiting a sick friend or comforting someone who has been hurt by life. I can't prove to you that any of those statements are true. I can only tell you that when you have learned to see the world in a certain way, you will accept them without requiring proof, and one of the lives whose specialness you will come to believe in is your own.

It is more than a matter of whether we look at a glass and see it as half full or half empty. It is whether faith and experience have taught us to look at a glass that is nearly empty, like Hagar's water bottle, and believe that there are resources in the world capable of refilling it.

There are certain things that happen to everybody. The sun comes up in the morning and fills the world with light. It sets in the evening and the world grows dark. In the course of the day, we grow hungry, find food to eat, and are satisfied. Weeks pass and the seasons change. We go through spells of feeling ill and recovering. We grow older and notice the changes in our bodies. Those around us grow older as well, and move in and out of our lives. People may once have believed that the sunrise, the rainfall, the successful harvest depended on their reciting certain prayers and performing certain rituals. (Many pagan societies would hold sexual orgies outdoors in the spring to ensure the fertility of the fields. Religious services were better attended in those days than they are today.) Now we know that sunrise and rainfall happen for reasons that have nothing to do with our praying or not praying. Our prayers and rituals don't affect the rainfall, but they do affect the way we see the rainfall. One person takes the availability of food for granted; another sees a miracle, a bounty which calls for admiration and gratitude. Once again, we respond as the person we are, not because of what happens but because of the way we have learned to see those happenings.

This leads us to what is perhaps the question of questions: Does the world make sense? Is nighttime a necessary and beneficial part of the rhythm of nature or is it a time of danger and chaos? Does it represent God's blueprint or God's absence? Is good health a person's normal condition and sickness an aberration, or is health a deceptive interlude while we wait for something else to go wrong? Is growing old and contemplating death part of God's design for us, or simply the result of our body wearing out and breaking down? I can't prove conclusively that the world makes sense; you can't prove conclusively that it doesn't. I can cite the regularity of the sunrise and sunset; you can call to witness earthquakes, floods, and droughts. I can marvel at the intricacy of the human body, the subtle sensitivity of the eye and ear, the brain, the respiratory system. You can counter with the body's vulnerability to disease and birth defects, so that even the finest mind or most graceful body can be completely undone by one tiny valve closing or a deficiency of one obscure enzyme.

Does the world make sense, or is it all a matter of chance? The facts won't prove the case either way. It comes down to the way we choose to see the facts: Is order the rule and chaos the exception? Or is chaos the rule and apparent order just a coincidence?

As with the previous question, my final argument derives not from facts but from the realities of the human soul: we seem to *need* to see the world as one that makes sense. As philosopher Suzanne Langer has written, a person "can adapt himself to anything his imagination can cope with, but he cannot deal with chaos." We have no trouble learning new things about the world as long as we can fit them into a previously existing frame of reference. (That may be why, in the sixteenth century, the church had so much trouble with

Copernicus and Galileo. It was not just a matter of the church admitting that it was wrong. Those scientists asked it to admit that its religious view of reality was wrong, which would have left it without a framework for understanding the world. The churchmen would not only have had to give up specific beliefs, which they probably could have managed to do, but would also have to give up their sense of what it meant to believe.) Whether the world makes objective sense or not, we need to believe that it does. We need to live in an intelligible universe. That is why we are simultaneously entertained and unsettled by horror movies and ghost stories in which the world suddenly stops behaving predictably. (We are entertained as long as we remember that we can leave the theater or put down the book and reenter the real, intelligible world.) The word we use for such books and movies is "uncanny." It means more than "weird." It refers to something not open to rational understanding—and that's a feeling we can only take in small doses.

We need to believe that the world we live in makes sense, that there is a pattern to it, and we look to religion to teach us that pattern. Long ago, people told stories of how God created the world, the sun and moon, the first human beings, as part of the process of persuading themselves that the world did make sense. It was their way of assuring themselves that there were reasons for everything that happened. We today have some of our questions answered by science (why weather behaves the way it does), some by psychology (why people behave the way they do). But behind the

everyday questions of meteorology and personal conduct stand the fundamental questions: Why is there a
world? Why did the human race come into being? Why
do people have thoughts, memories, longings? There
are no scientific answers to these questions. There is
only the answer of faith: you become a certain kind of
person when you choose to believe that there is a pattern and purpose to the universe, when you learn to see
the world through the eyes of faith. Certain things seem
worth making the effort to do, and others seem less
scary, when you have learned to see the world that way.
And both you and the world are better off for it when
you become that kind of person.

At the beginning of this century, the pioneering
anthropologist and sociologist Emile Durkheim traveled to the South Sea Islands to study religion in its
most primitive form. One of the important things he
learned is that the primary purpose of religion in early
societies was not to put individual people in touch with
God, but to put them in touch with each other. There
are events in the lives of each of us which we don't want
to have to face alone — joyous things like the birth or
marriage of a child, sad things like the loss of a parent,
frightening things like war or storms or natural disaster.
Religion teaches us to face them in the company of others, our neighbors around us and our ancestors before
us who faced similar situations and left records of their
experiences to enlighten and guide us. As anthropologist Edward Shils has written, "Rituals are systems of
belief directed toward . . . fortifying the individual to

face [danger] by affirming connections with the most fundamental realities . . . by interpreting the danger in such a way as to make it coherent with the universe as understood [by that religion]." In other words, religious ritual and the religious belief on which it is based cannot avert the danger, but they can help us face it bravely by teaching us that this is not the end of the world. If crops fail or buildings collapse, our religious perspective cannot magically make food appear or resurrect a building. But it can assure us that this is not a sign that laws of agriculture or gravity no longer apply. These are things that happen periodically, as they have happened to others, and we have learned ways of responding to them. They are unpleasant realities, but we can handle them so long as they are not evidence that we live in a haphazard, meaningless world.

Social psychologists who treated families in West Virginia in the aftermath of a devastating flood found that their gravest problem was not the loss of home or property. It was the loss of their sense that the world was a safe place. Long after they were settled in new homes with new furniture, they continued to have nightmares in which walls of water pursued them. It would take them years before they were able to trust the natural world again.

I imagine that all those West Virginia victims asked, "Why did the dam break and wipe out our homes?" At one level, the answer to the question would be a purely physical one. But somehow I don't think that was what they were asking. I don't think they really wanted to know how many cubic feet of water the dam was built to contain. I suspect they were really asking, "Can I trust the world? Can I go to sleep at night and not have to worry about being swept away in a flood? Do I live in a livable world or a treacherous one?" And those questions require not a scientific answer but a religious one.

Similarly, victims of crime, survivors of the Holocaust, refugees from some war-torn corner of the globe lose their ability to trust the world. They are haunted by the question "If people could do that to me once, what is to stop them from doing it to me again?" If they are not to spend the rest of their lives in fear, bitterness, and suspicion, they need to find a way of seeing the world that will not deny the tragic reality of what happened to them, yet will not compel them to see the world as a treacherous place. They will need a religious perspective which makes room for cruelty and suffering, yet affirms all that is good in the world.

Peter Berger, the outstanding sociologist of religion, sees the problem this way:

A child wakes up in the night, perhaps from a bad dream, and finds himself surrounded by darkness, alone, beset by nameless threats. . . . The child cries out for his mother. She will take the child and cradle him. . . . She will speak or sing to the child, and the content of this communication will invariably be the same: Don't be afraid—everything is in order, everything is all right. . . . All this belongs to the most routine experiences of life and does not depend upon any religious preconceptions. Yet this common scene raises a far-from-ordinary question which immediately introduces a religious dimension: *Is the mother lying to her child?* The answer can be No only if there is some truth to the religious interpretation of human existence. . . . The reassurance, transcending the immediately present two individuals and their situation, implies a statement about reality as such [Peter Berger, *A Rumor of Angels*].

In other words, we can close our eyes and go to sleep at night, we can teach our children to trust the world and not be afraid of the dark, of the shadows, of the thunder, only if we believe that "everything is all right." (Not literally *everything* of course, but enough for us to trust the world as a whole.) And we can only believe that when we have learned to look at the world, with all its pain and unfairness, through the eyes of faith. If the world is unreliable and people are basically untrustworthy, how could we ever turn our back on them, close our eyes and go to sleep?

Seeing life through the eyes of faith does something else for us. It enables us to see things that other people cannot see. When St. Paul in his Epistle to the Hebrews defines faith as believing in "the evidence of things not seen," I understand him to mean by that "things for which there is no proof." But I would take his words differently. To an objective observer, a Torah scroll is simply black ink on parchment. To me as a Jew, it is a symbol, a physical representation of the invisible point where God's will and human consciousness intersect. As such, it becomes immensely precious, worth much more than the parchment or the labor that went into writing it. That is why you will occasionally read of peo-

ple risking their lives to run into a burning synagogue to
rescue the Torah scrolls. This puzzles the person who
sees only objects and misses the "reality of things
unseen." (Hypothetical question: If your home were on
fire and you had time to save only one thing as you fled,
what would you grab? I bet it would not be the object
with the highest replacement price tag, but something
of great sentimental value. That is what it means to
evaluate things with eyes of love rather than by their
market price.)

To an objective observer, the cross is a simple geo-
metric design. To a Christian, it is a way of capturing
the subtle message of sacrificial love and the summons
to follow the hard road to salvation. A young woman
dying of cancer, the friend of a friend of mine, used the
imagery of the cross to describe what she was going
through, adding that religion gave her "a language to
describe what happens to me." Both the Torah and the
cross convey a message about God's reaching down to
express His love and concern for His creatures on
earth, but they convey that important message only to
the person who knows how to read the symbolic language of religion.

That is what a symbol does. It says something profound and important, but only to the person who has
learned to see the message in it. The wedding ring I
wear is more than a piece of jewelry; it is a symbol of
intimacy and loyalty. The flag I salute is more than colored cloth; it is a symbol of hundreds of millions of people, strangers to each other but connected to each other
by a shared vision of what our country stands for. Those

symbols elicit strong feelings in people only when they have been taught to read the messages hidden in the objects. Without that comprehension, the flag is only cloth, the scroll is only parchment. When religion has trained our eyes to recognize the reality of things not seen, those important messages disclose themselves to us.

I think I know which is God's favorite book of the Bible. I think it has to be the Book of Psalms. In the rest of the Bible, God speaks to us—through seers, sages, and prophets, through the history of the Israelite people. But in the Psalms, we speak to Him. We tell Him of our love, our needs, our gratitude.

I once debated a fundamentalist minister on television on some theological issues I had raised in one of my earlier books. He tried to prove a point about the innate sinfulness of human beings by quoting Psalm 51:7: "Indeed I was born in iniquity; in sin did my mother conceive me." I said to him, "Wait a minute. Even if you believe that the entire Bible is the word of God, accurately written down and accurately translated, it seems to me that you have to make an exception for the Book of Psalms. All those extraordinary poems of love and faith would be meaningless if God had written them to Himself. That would make God sound like the rock star who needed two full-time secretaries to handle his fan mail, one to write it and one to read it to him."

The Psalms are more than love poems God wrote to Himself. They are the emotional outpouring of people who learned to see the world through the eyes of religious faith. The world looks different to them than it does to the rest of us, and the inspired quality of their poetry flows from that difference. That is why, when I conduct a service or officiate at a funeral, I draw so heavily from the Psalms. They express my most profound feelings more eloquently than any words I could come up with myself.

(In 1972, I was writing my doctoral dissertation on the Book of Psalms and found that the work was playing tricks on my personal devotional life. I would be reading the Psalms as part of the morning prayers and would catch myself saying, "Now that's a communal lament, probably dating from the late First Commonwealth era, except for verse 7, which was added by a later editor." I had formed the habit of reading the Psalms through the eyes of a scholar and critic rather than those of a person hungry for God's presence. Only when I finished the dissertation could I go back to experiencing the Psalms instead of analyzing them.)

I envy the people who wrote the Psalms. (One thing I learned from my research was that King David did not write all one hundred fifty Psalms, and certainly not the ones about the Jewish exiles sitting by the waters of Babylon some four centuries after his death. He may have written some and been the patron of others, but like most Biblical authors, the psalmists did not put their names to their works.) I envy the psalmists the way I envy natural athletes and gifted musicians, for being able to do so well something that I would like to do well and find so hard. I envy them not only for their eloquence, but for the solidity of their faith and the clarity of their vision, their ability to find God in the sun and in the storm. Even when they complain to God, even when they cry out, "How long, O Lord, will You stand aside and let the wicked prosper?" they seem to believe totally in a God who cares about injustice, who hears prayer, and who has the power to set things right in the world. There are days when I have trouble believing that, days when I wonder about the efficacy of prayer and whether good will indeed triumph in the end. On days like that, I need to turn to the Psalms, not to find answers (I'm not sure their answers are that much better than mine or yours), not to be told what to believe, but to be reminded of what the world looks like when seen through the eyes of a believer.

Sometimes I find myself thinking that maybe the psalmists aren't that different from you and me. They may not have started out with remarkable spiritual gifts. They may simply have gone through experiences that brought to the surface whatever latent talent for religion they had. William James, in his classic work *The Varieties of Religious Experience*, writes of "once-born" and "twice-born" people. The once-born are people who sail through life without ever experiencing anything that shatters or complicates their faith. They may have financial problems, disappointments with their children, but they never go through a time when they say, "The religion I was raised in is a lie; that's not how the world works." Their understanding of God when they are old is not that different from their view of God when they

were children, a benign heavenly parent who keeps the
world neat and orderly.

James's twice-born souls are people who lose their
faith and then regain it, but their new faith is very different from the one they lost. Instead of seeing a world
flooded with sunshine, as the once-born always do, they
see a world where the sun struggles to come out after
the storm but always manages to reappear. Theirs is a
less cheerful, less confident, more realistic outlook. God
is no longer the parent who keeps them safe and dry;
He is the power that enables them to keep going in a
stormy and dangerous world. And like the bone that
breaks and heals stronger at the broken place, like the
string that is stronger where it broke and was knotted,
it is a stronger faith than it was before, because it has
learned it can survive the loss of faith. (I think of myself
as a twice-born, maybe even a three-times-born, person.
There are a lot of gods I used to believe in and no longer
do, because they proved false.)

Sometimes I suspect that great art—music, painting,
poetry—is only born out of great pain, the sort of pain
that shatters your old self, your old world-view, and
compels you to give birth to a new one. Sometimes I
suspect that the Psalms that move me most were not
written by people of serene, untroubled faith but by
people who had to struggle to find where God was hidden in their lives, not by people to whom God was obvi-
ous but by people for whom God was the reward at the
end of a long and arduous search.

Let me give you an example. Psalm 30, one of my
favorites, seems to have been written by a person who

has recovered from serious illness and offers the
Psalm perhaps to accompany a sacrifice in thanksgiving of his deliverance which he brings to the Temple.
He tells of how he used to take God's loving care for
granted, and assumed that as long as he was a good
person nothing bad would ever happen to him. Then
in a time of great trouble, he lost that simple faith and
replaced it with a more profound understanding of
God:

I will exalt Thee, O Lord, for Thou has lifted me up
And has not let my enemies make merry over me.
O Lord my God, I cried to Thee and Thou didst heal me.
O Lord, Thou has brought me up from Sheol
And saved my life as I was sinking into the abyss.
Sing a psalm to the Lord, all you His loyal servants,
And give thanks to His holy name.
In His anger is disquiet, in His favour there is life.
Tears may linger at nightfall, but joy comes in the morn-
     ing.
Carefree as I was, I had said, "I can never be shaken."
But, Lord it was Thy will to shake my mountain refuge;
Thou didst hide Thy face, and I was struck with dismay.
I called unto Thee, O Lord, I pleaded with Thee for
     mercy:
"What profit is there in my death if I go down into the
     pit?
Can the dust confess Thee or proclaim Thy truth?
Hear, O Lord, and be gracious to me; Lord, be my
     helper."
Thou has turned my laments into dancing,

Thou has stripped off my sackcloth and clothed me with
    joy,
That my spirit might sing psalms to Thee and never
    cease.
I will confess Thee forever, O Lord my God. [Psalm 30]

What do we know about the psalmist from his poem?
Apparently, he used to be a man who believed that
because he was a good, pious person, nothing bad
would ever happen to him (verse 6: "Carefree as I was,
I had said 'I can never be shaken' "). And for much of
his life that is exactly what happened. Then one day, his
world collapsed. He found himself desperately ill, at the
point of death, and his enemies were poised to rejoice
over his demise. He could not understand how this
could be happening to him. In his despair and confusion, he cried out to God, "Save my life, for Your sake if
not for mine. If I die, there will be one voice less on
earth to sing Your praises."

He recovers from his illness, and realizes that he has
learned three things from the experience. First (verse
5), God's absence from our lives is temporary ("Tears
may linger at nightfall, but joy comes in the morning").
His absence corresponds to the time we are giving birth
to a new soul, a new world-view to replace the simple
one which was stolen from us by circumstance. Losing
faith in a childish understanding of God is not the same
as losing faith in God.

Secondly, he learns from his experience that we worship God not because He will make our path smooth,
but because He gives us the grace and determination to

keep walking even when the path is rocky. God's promise is not that He will keep us from stumbling but that His hand will be there to help us get up again, no matter how often we stumble.

And finally, the psalmist learned that it is the task of the living person to praise God. (By implication, people who go through life without being grateful for health, food, friends, sunshine are, in a sense, dead.) Instead of being angry at God for letting him get sick, he feels he owes God something for his recovery, and he pays his debt by writing this Psalm, so that future generations will have the benefit of his experience (verse 12, "That my spirit may sing psalms to Thee and never cease").

The author of Psalm 30 did not become a religious poet because he led a charmed, safe, protected life. He became a religious poet by losing his faith and then finding it again (more accurately, by losing his faith and then finding a larger, stronger faith to replace it). He went through an experience many of us have gone through—he was very sick and got better—but where most of us go back to being the same person we were before the illness, he was changed by the experience. He learned how to see God in places he had never seen Him before.

As we continue our search for the differences that religion can make in the life of a good person, the extra dimension it can add, I would like from time to time to explore one or more of the Psalms with you. You, the reader of this book, deserve more than intellectual arguments for believing in God. You deserve the personal witness of people who started out questioning and ended up seeing this world as God's world.

True religion goes beyond making sense. It does not offend reason, it transcends reason. People do not start to see the world differently because someone has written a book giving them good reasons for doing so. They do it because they feel they have been touched by the presence of God—incarnated sometimes in words, sometimes in stories, sometimes in memories triggered by a written passage. Let me try to show you how the world looks when seen through the eyes of pure faith, how it looks to those who have learned to see things that we are blind to. For that, we can have no better guide than the Psalms.

3

PUTTING OUT THE SACRED FIRES

TO THE GEOLOGIST, MOUNTAINS ARE EVI-
dence of seismic activity, the process of reshaping the
earth's surface over the course of millennia. To the
tourist or traveler, mountains are sometimes beautiful,
sometimes inconvenient features of a landscape. To the
skier, snow-covered mountains are an opportunity to
enjoy a challenging outdoor activity. But to the religious
soul, a mountain is where God and human beings meet.
It represents earth reaching up to touch heaven, and
heaven bending down toward earth. So the ancient
Greeks and other peoples told stories of the gods living
atop the tallest mountains, and the Bible describes
Moses climbing a mountain to receive the Law from
God.

A few years ago, while my wife and I were vacation-
ing in the Pacific Northwest, at Mount Rainier
National Park, we heard the story of the first men who
ever climbed to the top of majestic Mount Rainier. In
the late nineteenth century, two pioneers found their

way west and were struck by the beauty of Mount Rainier. They felt challenged to conquer it, to climb to its peak. They sought to engage an Indian guide from one of the local tribes, but were told that the Indians considered it sacrilegious to climb the mountain. It was a sacred mountain, they were told, with a lake of fire at its top (there must have been memories of volcanic eruptions, as with nearby Mount Saint Helens), and they would not violate its sanctity by treading upon it. The climbers offered more and more money, and finally prevailed upon one Indian guide to help them. He sought at first to misdirect them, leading them up hills and down into valleys in the hope of tiring them out. But the two climbers were stubborn men, and kept going. Finally he led them a short way up the slopes of Mount Rainier and said to them, "I am forbidden to go any higher. From here on, you must go on alone." Bravely the men continued up the mountain, determined to reach the top. Finally they did. They planted a flag, took pictures of themselves at the summit, and returned the way they had come.

The park ranger who told us that story thought he was paying tribute to the courage and stubborn determination of two brave men. But the message I heard was a very different one. At one level, I had to admire their achievement, but at another, more profound level, I was saddened by their violation of a sacred precinct, their claiming for man what had previously been reserved for God. One of the things that modern men and women seem to do best is to put out sacred fires, extending the domain of men and shrinking the

domain of God, and I suspect that we a[...]
for it.

Once, there was magic and a sense of m[...]
lives. Once (in our childhood and in the childhood of
the human race), there were places that were unlike all
other places, and moments in time that were different
from ordinary time. They added color, texture, and
excitement to our lives. But today no place is off limits
to human ingenuity. We have become so good at unrav-
eling mysteries that few things still mystify us, and in
the process we may have become the people to whom
the late philosopher Joseph Campbell addressed this
warning: "When you get to be older and the concerns of
the day have been attended to, and you turn to the inner
life—well, if you don't know where it is or what it is,
you'll be sorry."

We have largely lost the capacity for reverence, the
sense of awe that comes from realizing how much
greater God is than we are. We have lost it, paradoxically, because the twentieth century teaches us both
how great we are and how small we are.

On the one hand, contemporary religion is less
inclined to cultivate feelings of reverence and awe in us
because it recognizes the need to reassure us of our
individual significance in a world that continually
brands us as insignificant. In the Middle Ages, people
built cathedrals, great soaring witnesses to the glory of
God. Walk into one of those cathedrals even today and
its unmistakable message is "God is great—and you,
human being, are small." But today, there are so many
secular settings which give us only the second half of

the message: "You, human being, are small and insignificant." We get it in department stores, airports, and bus
terminals. We get it in colleges and corporations where
we are known only to computers and identified by our
Social Security numbers. We get it at athletic stadiums
where we may be one of fifty thousand or a hundred
thousand anonymous spectators. At so many moments
of our lives, we are told that our presence doesn't really
matter. If we were not there, somebody else would be
there to take our place.

If you are a member of the "baby-boom generation,"
born between 1946 and 1962, this is the message you
have heard all your life. As part of a group, a demo-
graphic cohort, you were immensely powerful and
important. Advertisers neglected your parents (who
were paying the bills) and concentrated on you because
there were so many of you. When you were a teenager,
there was no end to the records and movies made for
teenagers. When you were a young adult, you were
inundated with movies and books dealing with young
adults' problems. As a member of that group you had
considerable clout. But as an individual, you never got
the sense that you mattered much. There was never
enough room for all of you. You went to junior high
schools that had not quite been completed, and high
schools that were overcrowded and unprepared for
you. The competition for good colleges and good jobs
was harder for you than it was for your older or
younger brothers and sisters because there were so
many of you.

The churches and synagogues of America recognized

your spiritual longing to be told that you mattered, that your presence or absence made a difference to somebody, and they shifted their focus from the majesty of God to the sacredness and importance of the individual. Emphasis on person-to-person relationships, on the difference one person can make, became important in church precisely because it was so rare elsewhere in our society. We stopped building cathedrals and built church and synagogue "boutiques," small, intimate houses of worship, instead. In the fifties, we were attracted to congregations of a thousand families or more. We wanted that sense of awe and confidence that came from being a member of God's mighty army. But in the seventies and eighties, because we were spending so much of our lives at school, at work, and at play being anonymous members of somebody's army, we wanted a different kind of religious experience. We saw the emergence of living-room churches and home Bible study groups. We saw the rise of *havurot,* small groups of families within synagogues, almost like large extended families, meeting to pray and celebrate. But in the process of celebrating the individual, the majesty of God and the reverence due Him somehow got lost.

But at the same time, ours has been a century of great human achievement—the conquest of distance, first through mass production of the automobile, then the jet plane, and of space, with the rocket to the moon; the near conquest of many illnesses with antibiotics, chemotherapy, organ transplants; the expansion of communication with radio, television, computers, satellites. We continually amaze ourselves with what we can do, and in the process God seems less and less impressive. When Samuel F. B. Morse invented the telegraph more than a hundred years ago, the first words he sent by wire were "What has God wrought!" When Neil Armstrong stepped onto the surface of the moon in 1969, his first words were "That's one small step for a man, one giant leap for mankind." Notice who gets the credit, and who gets left out, when it comes to twentieth-century marvels.

Technology is the enemy of reverence. Deliberately or inadvertently, technology puts out sacred fires because technology is the celebration of what man can do. In the Bible, idol-worship is not a matter of praying to stones and statues. Idol-worship is the celebration of the man-made as the highest achievement in the world. What is wrong with idol-worship, with worshiping human achievements as if they were the ultimate accomplishment, is not just that it is disloyal or offensive to God. The sin of idol-worship is that it is futile. Because it is really an indirect way of worshiping ourselves, it can never help us grow, as the worship of a God beyond ourselves can help us grow. As a result, we find life flat and uninspiring, and don't realize why.

Ultimately the worship of man and the celebration of the man-made becomes boring precisely because it cannot lift us beyond ourselves. There is something in us that intuitively understands this. We can look at a lake, at an ocean, at a mountain or meadow for hours on end and we do not feel bored; we feel peaceful and tranquil. But for how long can we look at anything man-made, a

jet plane, a skyscraper? Even the most elaborately pro-
duced television show begins to bore us after a while.

We tire of man-made things so quickly. Landing a
man on the moon is perhaps the greatest achievement of
twentieth-century technology. I remember the night of
the first moon landing. America came to a complete stop
that summer night in 1969. Restaurants and movie the-
aters were empty. City streets were deserted. We were
all home watching men make history. I also remember
the second time men walked on the moon. Few of us
stayed home to watch it. Our attitude was "What time is
it on? If I'm home and I remember, I'll tune it in.
Otherwise I'll catch it on the news tomorrow." For the
third lunar landing, the astronauts had to play golf on
the moon to get the networks to cover it, and before
long, space flights had become so routine that NASA
had to resort to gimmicks, sending first a senator, then
tragically a schoolteacher, into space to get people to
notice.

We who spend so much of our time in man-made
environments—cars, trains, schools, shopping centers,
office buildings—find life bland and uninspiring
because we are cut off from that contact with God's
world which used to draw us out of ourselves and fill us
with reverence as we responded to His presence.
Consider, for example, Psalm 8:

O Lord, how majestic is Your name throughout the
     earth . . .
When I behold Your heavens, the work of Your fingers,
The moon and stars that You have set in place,

What is man that You are mindful of him,
Mortal man that You take note of him? [Psalm 8:1, 3–4]

What is this sense of reverence, this special feeling we get when we contemplate the starry heavens, the soaring mountain, the awesome power of a blizzard or thunderstorm, this sense of seeing ourselves and our world differently because we have been in the presence of God? In 1917, the German theologian Rudolph Otto wrote his classic work *The Idea of the Holy*, which more than seventy years later remains the best introduction to the subject. He suggests that there is an overwhelming, almost frightening aspect to encountering the Holy. To meet it is to meet a reality so much greater than ourselves that we feel small in comparison, not because we are in fact small but because the Holy is great on a scale we have never known before.

Otto lists the ingredients of the encounter with the Holy as a sense of its majesty, its unapproachability, a feeling of fascination (we are scared but at the same time we want to draw closer), and what he calls "creaturely consciousness," the feeling that cannot be put into words but can only be experienced, the feeling that we are important enough to be invited to encounter the Holy but in its presence we are overwhelmed and made aware of our own smallness. Otto quotes Martin Luther to the effect that people have become so unaccustomed to the presence of God that they can no longer fear God properly, and he adds, "Modern man cannot even shudder properly."

What I find most important about our glimpses of the

Holy (a point that Otto touches on but does not stress as much as it needs to be stressed) is not simply that we learn there is a Power in the world much greater than our own power, but that we find that discovery, that shudder when we meet God, strangely comforting.

We want to believe in God. For all our celebration of our wondrous achievements, we don't really want to have ultimate responsibility for the world. Despite ourselves, we are deeply disappointed, even angry, when events make us wonder whether God is there for us or not. (I meet a lot of people who, in the face of personal tragedy or a major disaster, angrily conclude that there is no God. I am often struck by how angry some people get at God for not existing.) When we were children, we wanted to do things ourselves, we wanted the sense of mastery and achievement, but we needed the assurance that our parents were there because we knew we could do some things, more than we could have done six months or a year earlier, but we felt too small and weak to be left alone to do everything. Part of that feeling persists into our adult lives. No matter how much we achieve, no matter how complicated our machines or how destructive our weapons, when we contemplate the vast size of the world, we don't want to be the ones in ultimate charge of the whole project. The words of Psalm 8, "When I behold Your heavens, the work of Your fingers . . . What is man that You are mindful of him?" mean not only "How can You, O God, take notice of an insignificant creature like me in this vast world?" but also imply "How could it be conceivable that, in this vast universe, there is no Mind, no Power greater than the mind and power of a mortal human being like me?"

Let me give you two examples from everyday life that underscore this need, though our sense of reverence and awe has grown so weak that we don't recognize them for what they are. First, the next time you go to the zoo, notice where the lines are longest and people take the most time in front of the cage. We tend to walk briskly past the deer and the antelope, with only a passing glance at their graceful beauty. If we have children, we may pause with them to enjoy the antics of the seals and the monkeys. But we find ourselves irresistibly drawn to the lions, the tigers, the elephants, the gorillas. Why? I suspect that without realizing or understanding it, we are strangely reassured at seeing creatures bigger and stronger than ourselves, creatures we did not make and who are not subject to our control. It gives us the message, at once humbling and comforting, that we are not the ultimate power. Our souls are so starved for that sense of awe, that encounter with grandeur which helps to remind us of our real place in the universe, that if we can't get it in church, we will search for it and find it someplace else.

Second example: When I have to walk or drive in a snowstorm or a driving rain, I hate it. I find it uncomfortable, even dangerous. But when I am safe and warm inside my home, looking out at the thunderstorm or the falling snow, I respond very differently. I suspect we all do. For reasons my rational mind can't fully comprehend, it feels good to feel small and overwhelmed, but at the same time to be safe and protected, during the storm. It feels good, it is a welcome comfort to know that there is a Power in the world which far exceeds my own power or that of all people put together.

One of the oldest religious poems in existence is Psalm 29, in which the psalmist responds to a thunder-and-lightning storm by finding the majesty of God in the awesome might of the storm:

The voice of the Lord is over the waters,
The God of glory thunders,
The Lord is over the mighty waters.
The voice of the Lord is power, the voice of the Lord is
   majesty.
The Lord shatters the cedars of Lebanon . . .
While in His Temple, all say "Glory!" [Psalm 29: 3–5, 9]

I can picture the psalmist watching a storm move across the land, pelting the earth with rain, lighting up the dark sky with lightning flashes. His reaction is not "Wow, what a storm!" His reaction is like the religious person's reaction to the mountain or the tiger: "How great and mighty God must be to be able to create something like this." And more important, he is not only impressed; he is comforted by the sense that there is a God so great and powerful. The last line of the Psalm is:

May the Lord grant His people strength,
May the Lord bless His people with peace.

Because God has so much strength and power, He can supply us with the strength we need when we face challenges that exceed our human capacities.

Religion begins with a sense of reverence, the recognition of God's greatness and our limitations. That is why there are no atheists in foxholes and few atheists in hospitals. It is not because people are hypocrites, ignoring God when things are going smoothly and suddenly discovering Him and pleading piety when they are in trouble. And it is not just a matter of turning to God out of fear. There are no atheists in foxholes because times like those bring us face to face with our limitations. We who are usually so self-confident, so secure in our ability to control things, suddenly learn that the things that matter most in our lives are beyond our control. At the limits of our own power, we need to turn to a Power greater than ourselves.

People have always found God at the limits of their own strength. Farmers would pray for rain, soldiers would pray for victory, because they understood that no matter how well they did their job, they would need the favor of heaven for things to go well for them. But we today can barely see the limits of our own power. That leaves little room for God, and leaves us with the unwelcome sense of being in ultimate charge of this unmanageable mess we call the world. When we have succeeded in putting out all the sacred fires, where will we turn for warmth and light?

What do we lose when we lose the capacity for reverence? Let me ask what does not sound like a theolog-

ical question, but I believe it is: Why do we keep
tain parts of our bodies covered out of a sense
shame? Why is it acceptable for men to go around
bare-chested in hot weather but not for women? Why
are some people aroused, and others offended, when
movies or magazines show people displaying their private parts? The answer, I suspect, is not that sex is
dirty, but rather that sex is holy. Without realizing why
we feel what we feel, we have inherited that outlook
from ancestors who saw the presence of God in the
ability of a man and a woman to create life out of their
love for each other. The parts of the body which we
cover are the ones that contain the secret of generating
and sustaining life, and because the creation of life is
holy, we cover them out of an instinctive memory of
reverence. When we lose that sense of reverence (and I
am convinced that it is reverence for the life-force and
not modesty or physical vulnerability that is at work
here), when we become casual about nudity, we
become like animals, for whom mating and reproduction are purely a biological process. The holiness of life,
the holiness of love and birth, are lost to us when God
is factored out of the equation.

I disagree with those people who claim, sometimes on
religious grounds, that reproduction is the only legiti-
mate end of sexual activity. I believe that the expression
of love and intimacy, the transcending of the self to
become one with another person ("Therefore shall a
man leave his father and mother and cleave unto his
wife *and they shall become one flesh,*" Genesis 2:24), are
equally manifestations of holiness. That is why I per-

emonies for elderly couples and for
ically unfit to bear children. I find it
an beings are the only species who
ing sexual contact, because we are
species to whom it matters with whom we are
sharing the sexual act. But even as I disagree, I can
understand why some religious spokesmen say that the
purpose of sexual activity is not personal pleasure but
an encounter with holiness, and that this happens when
lovemaking leads to the miracle of conception and the
creation of a new life.

When doctors mastered the technique of fostering
conception in a test tube and implanting the embryo in
the mother's womb, many of those same religious conservatives were upset at the prospect of human beings
invading a realm that had previously belonged exclusively to God. Once more I disagree, insisting that we
do God's work when we remove a malignant tumor, set
a broken leg, or reverse infertility. But again, I understand their point of view. They are afraid that as human
beings learn to do what we have always credited God
with doing, we will lose our reverence for God and worship man instead, that we will revere science in place of
God. I may disagree with their position, but I share
their perception of the dangers involved.

One of the most sublime experiences we can ever
have is to wake up feeling healthy after we have been
sick. Even if it is only relief from a headache or
toothache, the health we take for granted most of the
time is suddenly seen to be an incredible blessing. If we

credit this return to health to our own recuperative powers or to the wonders of modern medicine, it will be just another encounter with technology in our lives, one more instance of idol-worship. But if we see the return to health as an encounter with God, as people used to do, as the author of Psalm 30 did (we read his story in the previous chapter), then we make room in our lives for reverence. We recover the capacity to see beyond ourselves. Our narrow, self-oriented world now has room for holiness in it.

A few years ago, the essayist and social observer Paul Fussell went to Indianapolis to watch the Memorial Day auto race at the Indianapolis Speedway. He was one of some 400,000 people watching what may well be the largest single-day single-location sporting event in the world, and he was there to try to understand what the appeal of the race was. The mood of the crowd, he found, was different from the mood of people who gather around an automobile accident. They were not there in the expectation of seeing someone injured or killed. "What takes place at Indy is not really a sport," he concluded:

> The essence of Indy is in its resemblance to other rituals in which wild, menacing, non-human things are tamed. I am thinking of the rodeo and the bullfight. Subduing beasts that, unsubdued, would threaten man—that is the ritual. . . . Indy enacts the ritual taming and domination of machines, emphasizing the crucial distinction between man and machines, the one soft and vulnerable but quick with courage and resource, the other hard and threatening

but witless and unimaginative. The cars at Indy are there so that men can be shown able to dominate them. . . . Indy is thus like a great Sunday morning proclamation of the dignity of man. . . . The reasons the extinction of the space shuttle *Challenger* was so distressing are many, but one was certainly the spectacle of the machine in that case winning. Those aboard lost their lives not to something like a hurricane or an earthquake but to a machine. The servant had suddenly turned master [Paul Fussell, *Thank God for the Atom Bomb*].

While one might argue with Fussell that the *Challenger* disaster was an instance of the machine's failure rather than its victory, emotionally I think he is right. We sense that something important is happening when a human being is pitted against technology, because we desperately need to be reassured that God's creation, man, is more wondrous than man's creation, the machine. From the legend of John Henry competing against the steam engine to the latest futuristic movie which pits a brave man against heartless technology, we sense how important it is for the machine to lose, not because we identify with the human hero, but because if our invention was mightier than God's invention, we would be displacing God, and we are not ready for that.

Elie Wiesel tells the story of the day man came before God on His heavenly throne and said to him, "Which do you think is harder, to be man or to be God?" "Being God is much harder," God answered. "I have a whole universe to worry about, planets and galaxies. All you have to worry about is your family and your job." "True enough," said man. "But You have infinite time and infinite power. The hard part is not doing the job, but doing it within the limits of human strength and the human life span." God answered, "You don't know what you're talking about. It's much harder to be God." Man replied, "I don't know how You can say that so confidently when You've never been human and I've never been God. What do You say we change places for just one second, so You can know the feeling of being man and I can know what it feels like to be God. Just for one second, that's all, and then we'll change back." God didn't want to, but man kept begging and pleading, and finally He relented. They changed places. Man became God and God became human. And the story goes on to say that, once man sat on the divine throne, he refused to give God back His place, and ever since then man has ruled the world and God has been in exile.

I don't believe that man really wants to be God. I suspect that, like the politician who enjoys winning the election more than he enjoys the hard responsibilities of public office, we enjoy being recognized for our success, our power, our creativity, but we don't really want to be in ultimate charge of the whole show. When problems are too hard for our minds to solve, when solutions are too long in coming for our mortal lives to encompass, we need to know there is Someone with more wisdom, more time, and more power than we have. The bedtime prayers we find in so many of our religious traditions are ways of saying "God, I can let myself relax and go to sleep because I know that the world doesn't totally depend on me. If I didn't have that faith, if I believed that everything depended on me, how could I ever neglect the world and go to sleep?"

In a century which encourages us to use computers and makes it so hard for us to write or read poetry, it is so easy to put out the sacred fires which have been tended for a hundred generations. It is so easy to dismiss religion as the residue of childish dependence and medieval ignorance. But if we do that, who will teach us to shudder? We will find ourselves turning to horror movies and tales of the supernatural, never understanding why we need them. Where will we find the reassurance that we need not despair when we run into a problem we can't solve? When the sacred fires have been extinguished, what will light our way to the encounter with the One in whose presence we come to understand our own potential greatness and our own ultimate creaturely consciousness?

CHAPTER

4

WHAT MAKES SOME THINGS WRONG?

A RABBI IS A TEACHER. I TEACH IN MANY ways, formally and informally, by precept and by example. Some years ago, I taught a class in modern Jewish history for teenagers in my congregation. We spent a lot of time on the Holocaust, the destruction of six million Jewish men, women, and children at the hands of the Nazis because they were Jews. As we read example after example of sadism, butchery, and cruelty, I could see the cumulative outrage in the souls of my students reaching the boiling point. They were so angry at what had been done to helpless victims not long before they were born, in some cases in countries where they might well have lived if their grandparents had not left Europe for America.

When we were done studying the history of those years, I asked them, "Why was Hitler wrong?"

They were confused by my question. "What do you mean, why was Hitler wrong?" one student asked incredulously. "Do you mean he may have been right, that the Jews were an inferior race and should be murdered?"

Another cried, "Why was he wrong? You can't just take people and kill them because you don't like them!"

"Remember," I pointed out to them, "the Nazis were careful to pass laws sanctioning everything they did. It was all within the law. Was it still wrong?"

"Well, of course it was," the first student replied. "You can't pass laws permitting the gassing of little children just because they're Jewish."

"Are you trying to tell me that some things are wrong even if a majority of the people think they are right? Are you telling me that there is such a thing as right and wrong built into the human conscience, and it's not just a matter of how you feel about it?"

Again they looked confused, and one finally answered, "Well, yeah, I guess so. I never thought about it that way before."

The affirmation of monotheism—that there is only one God—is a moral statement, not a mathematical deduction. If there is only one God and He demands moral behavior, then there can be such a thing as good and evil. (Technically speaking, right and wrong are matters of fact: Who stole the money? Good and bad are matters of morality: Should I take the money?) When there are many gods, as in pagan legends, the issue is not: What is good? The issue is: Which God shall I serve? Which one has the power to protect and reward me? Think, for example, of the conflicts in Homer's *Iliad*, where the gods take sides. What pleases one displeases another. A person offends one of the gods but is under the protection of another, stronger one. The issue is not what is right but who has the might.

The assertion that there is only one God is the assertion that issues of moral behavior are not matters of personal taste. We cannot decide by majority vote that it is all right to steal and lie, any more than we can decide that winters should be mild or cookies more nourishing than vegetables. Bertrand Russell, perhaps the most articulate spokesman for enlightened atheism in our generation, captured the dilemma with which I confronted my Holocaust students in these words: "I cannot . . . refute the arguments for the subjectivity of ethical values, but I find myself incapable of believing that all that is wrong with wanton cruelty is that I don't like it." In other words, it may be hard to persuade someone philosophically that there is a God who sets moral standards for us. We may be more comfortable with the notion "I will do what I believe is good, and I will leave you free to do what you believe is good." But we instinctively feel that there is something lacking in our philosophy when it can be reduced to "Personally, I choose not to torture little children or persecute people because of their race or religion, but if it doesn't bother you to do it, go ahead."

As I see it, there are two possibilities. Either you affirm the existence of a God who stands for morality and makes moral demands of us, who built a law of truthfulness into His world even as He built in a law of gravity (so that if we violate either one, we suffer the consequences). Or else you give everyone the right to decide what is good and what is evil by his or her own lights, balancing the voice of one's conscience against the voice of temptation and need, like some cartoon character with an angel whispering in one ear and a devil whispering in the other.

Some moral philosophers distinguish between two kinds of wrongdoing. There are things which are wrong because people have declared them wrong, like driving over the speed limit or on the wrong side of the road, and there are things which are wrong in and of themselves, like murder or rape. What makes them wrong? Not public opinion (it might be possible to get 51 percent of the population to vote in favor of permitting adultery or letting the poor steal from wealthy corporations); they are just wrong whether people like it or not.

Which brings me to my problem with Clint Eastwood. I have seen only one of his very successful "Dirty Harry" movies, but I remember it clearly. I have never responded to a movie the way I did to that one, with as strong a sense of divergence between my mind and my gut. Throughout the movie, my head kept saying, "Why am I watching this? This is cheap, manipulative trash." But at the gut level, my emotional reaction was "Yeah, go get 'em. Get out the Magnum and blast them away. Don't let those punks get away with it." Intellectually, I found it shallow. Emotionally, I found it compelling and satisfying.

The point is not that the millions of people who go to Clint Eastwood movies are less intellectual and more emotional than I am. The point is that there is something instinctive in me, and I suspect in every one of us, that reacts with a surge of anger to injustice, to the prospect of villains and criminals "getting away with it." It is not an intellectual position, a carefully thought out conclusion about what kind of society I want to live in. It is a gut reaction, an instinctive sense of "That's not right." (I can't tell you how many people have urged me to write a book on the problem of "when *good* things happen to *bad* people.")

Edmund Cahn, former professor of law at New York University, suggests that there is such a thing as a "sense of injustice." We may not be able to define justice, he writes, but we all recognize injustice when we see it, and we all respond to injustice in the same way, the way I responded to the villain in the Clint Eastwood movie, with a feeling of outrage and a sense of "That's not fair." Even little children are capable of saying "That's not fair" (and not only about what happens to them, but also about unfair treatment of friends or even strangers).

This sense of injustice is more than a matter of maintaining a safe society. It is not saying it is wrong to steal because it would be maddening to live in a society where other people could take your belongings. It is not saying we should not murder because if it were all right to murder, the people with the most guns would control the world, and they might not be the best people to do that. It says murder and theft are wrong. Even if you could persuade yourself that the world would be better off if certain people were killed, or if the poor could take what they need from the rich because they need it more, it would still be wrong. Codes of law before the time of Moses were phrased "If a man kills another, this will be his punishment. . . . If a man steals, this is the punishment." The Ten Commandments were the first code to go beyond "If . . . then . . ." and say "You shall not murder! You shall not steal!" not because it is punishable, not because it is illegal, but because it is wrong.

Where does our sense of injustice come from? I would maintain that it comes from God, by which I mean that it is not man-made, not a matter of human consensus, but is built into the world we live in, as part of what makes it a world capable of morality.

Furthermore, just as I believe that our encounter with holiness is something we welcome, so I would maintain that our encounter with the moral dimension of life, the existence of fixed standards of good and evil, is not just something we recognize, like the truth of a geometrical proposition, but something we have reason to be grateful for. I believe we want to be addressed by God. We want to be recognized as moral beings, significantly different from animals because we have eaten from the Tree of Knowledge of Good and Evil. We want to have moral demands made of us, not because we are sure we will live up to them, but because the demands addressed to us make us feel that we are special because we are human.

Think of it this way: Can you remember when you were in high school and you stayed up all night working on a homework project because you wanted it to be perfect? A week later, when you got it back and it was clear that the teacher had hardly looked at it but had just checked it off as having been handed in, how did you feel? I suspect you felt, "What's the point of working so hard to do a good job if nobody cares? Next time, I'll do the least I can get away with, and spend the rest of my time watching television."

We want to know that we are taken seriously. We want to feel that our decisions—to lie or not to lie, to steal or to respect other's property—are important at the highest level. The idea that standards of good and evil are set by God, and do not come from within ourselves, gives us that message.

Unitarian minister G. Peter Fleck recalls seeing a drama on television in which a man dies and finds himself standing on line, addressed by a bored usher who tells him he can choose either door, the one on the right leading to heaven, the one on the left leading to hell.

"You mean I can choose either one?" the man asks. "There is no judgment, no taking account of how I lived?"

"That's right," the usher says. "Now move along, people are dying and lining up behind you. Choose one and keep the line moving."

"But I want to confess, I want to come clean, I want to be judged."

"We don't have time for that. Just choose a door and move along."

The man chooses to walk through the door on the left, leading to hell.

Fleck's conclusion is that "in the end, we want to be held accountable . . . we want to be judged and ultimately to be forgiven."

My grandfather was a house painter in Lithuania,

eking out a modest living. But in addition to his public life as a house painter, he had a secret identity. He was one of God's agents on earth, maintaining literacy in a sea of ignorance and kindness in a world of cruelty. His days, his every act became important because he believed it mattered to God what he ate, how he earned and spent money, how he respected his wife and treated his children. That sense of having to live up to God's standards redeemed my grandfather's life from anonymity and insignificance, and it can do the same for each of us.

I am bothered about the school of thought that has emerged in recent years and has come to be known as New Age theology. The term covers a lot of trends, some of which have very little in common with each other but are connected in the public mind. The interest in New Age spirituality includes everything from meditation and holistic medicine, which I respect and take seriously, to a belief in reincarnation à la Shirley MacLaine, about which I try to keep an open mind, to a belief in the healing power of crystals and the ability of people to read the future through tarot cards, which I can't understand anyone taking seriously. Although there are no systematic New Age theologians, a fairly coherent world-view has begun to emerge, a strange blend of partially digested Buddhism and post-Einsteinian physics. Its basic beliefs seem to be these:

—The God we read about in the Bible and learned about in Sunday school does not exist. "God" is more accurately described as a source of energy within the universe. If we can learn to tap into that energy, we can enhance our lives.

—An iron law of fate (sometimes called karma, the Buddhist term) rules our lives. We get what we deserve in life, or sometimes we get in this life what we earned on the basis of our behavior in a previous incarnation.

—There are no accidents. Nothing comes into our life unless we invite it in consciously or subconsciously. Louise Hay, in her best-selling book *You Can Heal Your Life*, goes so far as to identify what your spiritual failings must be on the basis of what disease you come down with or where a malignant tumor is located. Thus blacks get sickle-cell anemia and homosexuals and drug addicts get AIDS because of their self-destructive belief that they are "not as good as other people." Hepatitis stems from "resistance to change" and multiple sclerosis, she writes, stems from "mental hardness, hard-heartedness, iron will, inflexibility and fear."

Diane, a young, attractive aerobics instructor I met, told me why she saw life that way and why she disagreed with the view of misfortune and tragedy I had written about in my book *When Bad Things Happen to Good People.* "I believe nothing happens to you unless you secretly want it to," she told me. "Last week, for example, I was driving to work. I was stopped at a traffic light when a careless driver hit me from behind, causing major damage to my car. I said to myself, Now why did this happen to me? Then I remembered that, just two days before, my father called to tell me he was buying a new car and trading in his two-year-old Lincoln Continental. My first thought was, Why doesn't he give me the Lincoln instead? But he won't, because I've got a perfectly good car. Then two days later, the car I wished I didn't have was totaled in an accident. Are you going to tell me that was just a coincidence?"

"Diane," I said, "let's accept the premise that you wanted to be rid of your car. Did the driver who hit you want to be rid of his car too? Is that why he ran into you? Did the insurance company subconsciously want to be rid of the several thousand dollars the accident ended up costing them?"

"They must have," she answered. "Otherwise why did it happen?"

"What about the two hundred passengers on an airplane that crashes? What about all the children who are born with birth defects? Are those things that they wanted to have come into their lives?"

She looked puzzled for a moment, then said, "Well, maybe they had been cruel or vain in a past life, and this was a lesson they needed to learn." Her answer reminded me of a story the late comedian Sam Levenson used to tell. The day he started first grade, his mother came and said to the teacher, "If my boy Sammy misbehaves, hit the kid next to him. He learns by example."

But that interpretation of misfortune is not my main source of discomfort with New Age religion. My main problem is that when God is seen as "energy," religion becomes a one-way process: we demand and get things from God, but God neither demands nor receives anything from us. For me (and I would insist, for the

Bible), the essence of a relationship with God is the notion of Covenant. Just as a child one day reaches the point where his parents say to him, "We're not going to treat you like an infant anymore, responding to you because you cry, giving you what you want simply because you want it; from now on, we will have expectations of how you will behave as a member of this family," so God one day said to the human race, "You have matured to the point where I can tell you My expectations of you. No more responding to you because you are weak and needy; now I expect you to be kind, honest, and truthful."

As the Bible says, "For the land you are about to possess is not like the land of Egypt, out of which you came, where you sowed your seed and watered it by foot like a vegetable garden. The land you are going to possess is . . . a land the Lord your God cares for. The eyes of the Lord are upon it, from the beginning of the year until its end" (Deuteronomy: 11:10–12). In other words, in the place you lived until now, God sent you water to make the crops grow whether you deserved it or not. But in the future, you will be rewarded only if you deserve it. The eyes of God will be upon your society, to see if you live up to His expectations.

For me, the one thing that defines us as human beings is this metaphor of the eyes of God being upon us. I don't take that phrase literally. I don't literally believe that God has eyes with which He watches us. (If I did, I would have to wonder what color God's eyes are.) Rather, I take it to mean that God makes moral demands of us, that there are standards by which God summons us to live. For me, that verse from Deuteronomy is bad meteorology—I have no reason to believe that the rain falls only on the farms of the virtuous; but it is good theology—we are summoned to live at a higher level by the notion that our behavior matters to God.

Charles Darwin was once asked, after all his discoveries about how we are linked to the lower animals, whether there was still anything unique about being human. He answered, "Man is the only animal that blushes." (To which Mark Twain added, "Sure, man is the only animal with good reason to blush.") What does it mean to blush? It is an expression of self-consciousness, of knowing that we are being watched and being held to standards. In the Bible, the first thing that happened to Adam and Eve after they ate the forbidden fruit of the Tree of Knowledge of Good and Evil was that "their eyes were opened and they knew that they were naked." The other animals in the garden were equally naked, but were unaware of it. One of the results of a knowledge of good and evil is the feeling of self-consciousness, the sense that Someone is watching you.

Sigmund Freud, when asked if he could summarize the whole theory of psychoanalysis in one sentence, answered in six words: where id is, let ego be. That is, psychoanalysis tries to bring us to the point where we can substitute choice for impulse. It may be the most religious thing that old demolisher of religious icons ever said. If I were asked to summarize the moral thrust of the Bible in one sentence, it would come out remarkably like what Freud said: don't do what you feel like doing; do what God wants you to do.

For me, New Age religion infantilizes our relationship with God. It would take us back to the pre-moral stage of religion, asking for something, trying to manipulate God to get what we want, without our having to meet any standards at our end of the relationship. In a sense, it is "yuppie religion," a theology for impatient, narcissistic souls, promising that you can have something, not because you have earned it but simply because you want it.

But does that make it wrong? Let us consider what we lose when we hear only the side of religion which teaches us to say "Give me" and are deaf to the religious voice that demands righteousness of us. Psalm 119 is long, 176 verses, the longest single chapter in all of Scripture. In its Hebrew original, it takes the form of an acrostic, a poem whose lines follow the letters of the alphabet, with eight lines for each of the twenty-two letters of the Hebrew alphabet. I admire the determination of the psalmist trying to say something fresh and original in that confining format, and when I make the effort to read it closely, I find it contains a great spiritual truth. It is a love song of praise for God's law:

Teach me, O God, the way of Your laws,
I will observe them to the utmost.
Give me understanding that I may observe Your teaching
And keep it wholeheartedly . . .
O how I love Your teaching,
It is my study all day long.
Your commandments make me wiser than my enemies;

They always stand by me.
I have gained more understanding than my elders,
For I observe Your precepts . . .
Your word is a lamp to my feet,
A light for my path.
I have firmly sworn to keep Your rules.
  [Psalm 119:33–34, 97–98, 100, 105–106]

We modern people tend to be uncomfortable with laws. We see them as confining, taking away our freedom. I sometimes think the essence of the modern outlook is "This is a free country, and nobody is going to tell me what to do." (In my home state of Massachusetts, voters recently defeated a proposed mandatory seat belt law, not because they believe in their inalienable right to injure themselves while driving, but simply because they didn't want the government telling them what to do, even if it was clearly for their own good. They feel they have to live with enough rules already.) Our love of freedom makes it hard for us to understand someone like the author of Psalm 119 who speaks of loving the law and being grateful for it. The psalmist loves the law first because the sense of being commanded assures him that God takes him seriously, and also because he is happier living in a world where people feel addressed and summoned by God. It is law that keeps us from returning to the jungle, to a situation where the strongest take what they want. It is law that keeps us human, guiding us to the realization that there are greater callings and higher satisfactions in life than constantly looking out for our own self-interest.

Just as the world would be unlivable if we could not count on the reliability of the law of gravity and other laws of chemistry and physics, the world of our social relationships would be unlivable if we could not accept certain standards of behavior as being right and necessary even when we do not feel like living up to them. It is hard enough to do what is right. How much harder would it be if we first had to figure out what was right, and then summon the moral energy to do it? As Robert Bellah and his colleagues write in *Habits of the Heart,* "It is the moral context of relationships that allows marriages, families and communities to persist with some certainty that there are agreed-upon standards of right and wrong that we can count on and that are not subject to incessant renegotiation."

A character in Dostoevsky's *The Brothers Karamazov* says, "If there is no God, everything is permitted." I think he means more than simply "If there is no one to hold me accountable and punish me, I can do whatever I want." I suspect he means "Without God, what makes something I do wrong? It may be illegal. It may be distasteful to you. It may hurt people who don't deserve to be hurt. But if I feel good doing it, what makes it *wrong?*"

The moral relativist, the person who believes that something is right if you feel it is right, may feel free in his rejection of absolute standards of good and bad, but his freedom is the freedom of the sailor at sea without a compass. He is free to choose to travel in any direction he fancies, precisely because he has no way of knowing which direction the harbor lies in. Should we envy him that sort of freedom? James Webb, a Marine Corps Vietnam veteran who later served as Secretary of the Navy, once wrote, "Mine has not been a generation that offered its children certainties. We have treated them to endless argument instead. . . . Our children in many cases have grown up under the false illusion that there are no firm principles, that for every cause there is a countercause, for every reason to fight there is a reason to run." To deny that God is the author of moral standards not subject to human ratification is to deny the instinctive voice inside each of us that reacts to the Clint Eastwood movie, or to the latest real-life atrocity in the news, by saying "That's not right." We mean more than "I wouldn't want that to happen to me" or even "I wouldn't want to be a person who does such things." We mean "Nobody should do such things!" And what answer, if not God, do we have to the person who says "Why not?"

This, then, is what I believe:

There are absolute standards of good and evil built into the human soul. I describe them as "God-given," though I cannot understand the process by which God communicated them to us any more than I can ever understand where an idea or an inspiration comes from. Moses may have gotten his ideas about morality from the same place that Shakespeare got his poetry and Mozart his music, but the process surpasses my understanding. I describe them as "God-given" to convey the idea that they are a permanent part of life, not subject to human approval or disapproval.

We know only imperfectly what those standards are,

but our knowledge of them is constantly growing. Issues of slavery and the dignity of women and children, issues of freedom of thought and belief, are clearer to us now than they were a century or two ago. The fact that we have not found all the answers does not mean that answers don't exist.

Not everything is morally good or bad. There is no moral dimension to how long a man's hair or a woman's skirt should be. There may not even be moral guidelines on drinking alcoholic beverages in moderation. (No moral code approves of drunkenness, but some religions forbid alcohol entirely, some command it on certain occasions, and others take no position.) But how we relate to other people and how we learn to control our basic instincts *are* subjects for moral guidance.

The fact that different societies have different moral codes does not mean that one is as good as another. If Eskimos used to leave elderly parents to die when they become economic burdens, or if the ancient Greeks put handicapped children to death, I am not obliged to say, "When in Nome, do as the Eskimos do." I need not agree that the rights of the elderly or the handicapped are matters of local custom. I would say instead that economically marginal societies sometimes have to do things that are wrong in order to survive, even as soldiers and policemen sometimes have to kill people to protect society as a whole, but that does not call the dignity and sanctity of human life into question. I know that there are some societies where extramarital sex is casually accepted, but I can't help feeling that people in those societies will grow up missing out on some of the

most profound rewards human life and love have to
offer.

I can think of several ways in which we are helped
by grounding these standards of good and bad in religion. The first is through what we call revelation.
Without pretending to understand this process, I
believe that the authors of the Bible capture God's will
on moral issues better than any other source. But it was
God's first word on the subject, not His last. The last
word has not been heard yet. We can feel that we have
gone beyond the promise of reward and the threat of
punishment which we find in parts of the Bible, and we
have learned (in large measure from the pages of the
Bible itself) to be uncomfortable with its commands to
stone Sabbath-breakers or kill Amalekites. But even
the most dedicated atheist or secular humanist would
have to admit that the moral values he cherishes derive
from, and his conscience has been formed by, the
Biblical heritage.

Beyond revelation, we have tradition, thousands of
years of insight, experience, trial-and-error carried out
by people of profound spiritual sensitivity and caring.
The Judaism I practice is not the religion of the
Hebrew Bible, the Old Testament. The Christianity my
neighbor practices is not the religion of the New
Testament. In both cases, we have added the fruits of
centuries of experience and innovation to the Scriptural
base. To draw our moral values from religious tradition
and experience is to spare each generation the burden
of starting from scratch. I am guided in my ethical deci-
sion-making not only by the voice of my own con-

science but by the voices of many before me, wiser and more insightful than my own.

And finally, grounding my moral response in God gives me the confidence that what I am committed to is not only my opinion or the opinion of my parents, teachers, and childhood heroes. There is something profoundly, permanently *right* about it. When I waver in my commitment, when I am on the verge of backing away from doing what I believe because it is hard, unpopular, or expensive, I need to know that my path is God's path.

CHAPTER

5

MORE DIE OF LONELINESS

IN A COMMUNITY NOT FAR FROM MINE, there lived a widow who had three grown sons. Two of them married and moved away. The third stayed home to take care of their mother. The mother was in her late seventies, the son was fifty, and everyone assumed that after the mother died, the son would finally get on with his life. But things seldom work out as we assume they will. One day, the son had a heart attack and died. The mother was distraught. Deprived of her constant companion and caretaker, she grew increasingly depressed and confused. Cooking and cleaning became too much for her. Her two remaining sons flew home to deal with the problem. They began to check out nursing homes, and took her to visit one where her seventy-nine-year-old cousin had been living. Unfortunately, the cousin had only a long list of complaints about the food, the other residents, the staff. Then out of the blue, one of the women (they can no longer remember which one thought of it first) had the idea that the cousin leave the home and move in with the widow. The results were startling. Like a parched plant that people begin to water, the widow seemed to grow younger and healthier daily. Having someone to share her life with, someone who needed her, gave her back her reasons for living. She had been on the verge of dying of loneliness, and now she had reasons to get up in the morning and look forward to the new day.

More than any other human problem, loneliness, the absence of meaningful human connection, drains the joy and the sense of purpose from our lives. It explains why people go to shopping centers who have no intention of shopping—they just need to be somewhere where other people are, hoping that among the hundreds of strangers going by they will find one familiar, friendly face. It is why people come home from work or school and immediately turn on the television. They are not interested in the program; much of the time, they don't even know what is on. But they are desperate for the sound of another human voice in their lives. Saul Bellow called his most recent novel *More Die of Heartbreak.* I would change it to say that, in my experience, more die of loneliness.

Many lonely people believe that if they could only meet and marry the right person, that would cure their loneliness. Think of all the best-sellers about relationships, about why people can't love or why they love too much. These books, aimed almost exclusively at women with the message "Buy me, read me, and you will find a man to solve your problem," strike me as more elaborate versions of the toothpaste and shampoo ads with their message "Buy me, use me, and you will find a man to solve your problem." They feed into our fairy-tale fantasies of prince and princess meeting, kissing, and riding off into the sunset to live happily ever after.

Yet the sad truth is that even married people can be lonely and unconnected. It is a dangerous mistake to depend on one person to meet all of our emotional needs. That is asking a lot of one person (who probably has his or her own problems with intimacy, dependence, and fears of loneliness), and almost inevitably leads to a frustrating cycle of unrealistic expectation, inevitable disappointment, and undeserved anger.

How did we get into this situation where, in a world full of more people than ever before and with entire industries dedicated to making us happy, so many people find themselves lonely and unhappy? I think the reasons for our plight are individualism, the myth of independence, and the competitiveness which is at the heart of our culture.

We have made the twentieth century the century of the individual. For most of human history, a person was part of a family, part of a clan or tribe or neighborhood. People defined themselves on the basis of their relationships to other people, not on the basis of their individual achievements. Think of all those pages the Bible devotes to genealogies, lists of who descended from whom. Remember how confused we would become when reading a Russian novel, because one character would address another as "Misha son of Ivan" instead of calling him by the formal name with which we had first been introduced to him.

But today a family is no longer a unit. It has become a collection of units living at the same address but all of them coming and going, eating and sleeping on separate schedules. Because the family is no longer a unit but a collection of individuals, we can read of a child suing his parents for raising him badly, or a wife suing her husband for not shoveling the snow off the front steps, causing her to fall and injure herself. In another age, the idea of one family member suing another for negligence would have been unthinkable. But today we assume that the family, town, occupation, or social class you were born into are simply circumstances you can choose to leave behind as you pursue your own well-being.

(I don't know if it really happened or not, but I heard this story about one of the inventors of the transistor. He was driving to a conference where he was to be honored for his invention, and on the way he stopped for lunch at a roadside fast-food establishment. At one of the tables, he saw a family—mother, father, and two teen-age children—each listening to a transistor radio with a set of earphones on, not one of them saying a word to anyone else, each totally in his or her own world. He left the restaurant wondering if mankind might not have been better off without his invention.)

Psychotherapy, the "talk cure" that is many people's chosen instrument for getting happy, also focuses on the individual in order to maximize happiness. I recall reading an article by a psychiatrist who commented that she had heard many of her colleagues boast of having made patients more assertive, more independent. She didn't remember ever hearing one boast of having made a client more charitable, more nurturing. A comprehensive survey of mental health in America states, "Psychoanalysis (and psychotherapy) is the only form of psychic healing that attempts to cure people by detaching them from society and relationships. All other forms—shamanism, faith healing, prayer—bring the community into the healing process, indeed use the interdependence of patient and others as the central mechanism in the healing process" [Veroff, Kulka, and Douvan, *Mental Health in America*].

Some therapists have come to acknowledge that none of us lives in a vacuum. They have begun to practice couples therapy, recognizing that the relationship, not either of the individuals, is their patient. They see the family as a self-contained system, rather than a bunch of healthy individuals trying to cope with a neurotic relative. But many therapists, and many books of "pop psychology," still convey the message that "you have to make the most of your own life, and if that means leaving behind people who have come to depend on you, that's too bad. Let it be a growing experience for them." The result, not surprisingly, is that we have a lot of people who have learned to grab what they believe they have coming to them but are blind to the needs of others; people see love and sex as areas of conflict and conquest rather than sharing and intimacy, and go through life feeling that other people are withholding that which would make them happy.

One of the benefits of being a clergyman is that I can live near where I work. My synagogue is just over a mile from my house, and unless the weather is brutal or my schedule hectic, I can walk to my office. But every now and then I have to drive to Boston for a meeting or to the airport on the other side of town. On those occasions, I am reminded of what most people have to go through twice a day. The highways and city streets are clogged with cars, most of them containing only one person, inching along, overheating, frustrating their drivers. It is the ultimate outcome of our culture of individualism. Everyone wants the convenience of being in his own car, and as a result everyone suffers, everyone is angry and frustrated.

That splendid writer Joanne Greenberg has written a short story, "Merging Traffic," in which her narrator, an emergency medical technician who pulls injured people out of wrecked cars, uses the highway as a metaphor for life. Each of us goes through life in our own self-contained bubble, trying to avoid contact with other people in their bubbles, feeling indignant if anyone should violate the privacy of our individual space. In the words of Philip Slater, whose book *The Pursuit of Loneliness* may be the best book written on the subject, "Even within the family, Americans are unique in their feeling that each member should have a separate room, and even a separate telephone, television and car when economically possible. We seek more and more privacy, and feel more and more alienated and lonely when we get it."

Slater may be right in saying that this is more of a problem in America than in other cultures, because this country was founded on an ideology of rugged individualism. Americans today, with the exception of a few thousand Indians, are not the descendants of a native population but of people who left their homelands to cross an ocean in search of something better, and who settled the continent by again leaving home and friends behind and moving farther west. To face the frontier alone was heroic; to need the support system of civilization was somehow seen as a weakness. My father, who left his native Lithuania at the age of eighteen, knowing that he would probably never see his parents again, was typical of the immigrant story that began with the Pilgrims and continues today with Asian and Central American immigrants. And even today, Americans respond to the siren song of independence. A recent Boston Sunday *Globe* featured a special section on franchise opportunities, with the typical American message "Why work for someone else? You can be your own boss."

To be an American is to be raised on the myth that a real American is ready to leave security behind and set out on his own in search of fame and fortune. It has led to some very impressive results, but it has also led to a lot of rootless, lonely, detached people. We move away from our families and support systems, and then we look for ways to fill that gap. So Americans become almost compulsive joiners—Elks, Rotary, Masonic Lodges, bowling teams—in an effort to replace the family they left behind. It helps, but it doesn't quite do the job. No matter how active we become, or how much we like the other people in the organization, we can never quite forget that the association is an artificial one. We can walk away from it at any time, and so can the other members, and that makes our bonds with them that much more tentative. To cite Philip Slater again, "Much of the unpleasantness, abrasiveness, and costliness of American life comes from the fact that we are always dealing with strangers. . . . Individualism is rooted in the attempt to deny the reality of human interdependence."

Along with individualism and independence, another element in society's unwitting conspiracy to leave us lonely is the competitiveness with which we conduct our lives. We have been taught to see life as a race in which prizes are given only to those who finish first. (In the spring of 1988, my wife and I traveled to visit her parents in Omaha, Nebraska. On the way, we saw a number of people wearing T-shirts that read "University of Kansas, NCAA Championship 1988—We're Number One!" We didn't see any that said "University of Oklahoma—We Finished a Close Second!" One of my favorite trivia games is to see how far back people can remember losing presidential candidates, men who received the support of forty to fifty million votes but did not win, and are therefore losers consigned to the dustbin of history.) As a result, we tend to see everyone around us as a potential rival, a person who wants to take away from us what will make us successful and therefore happy. Our gain has to mean their loss and vice versa.

On a speaking trip to the West Coast, I heard this story about a bright young man, a pre-med sophomore at Stanford University. To reward him for having done so well in school, his parents gave him a trip to the Far East for the summer vacation between his sophomore and junior years. While there he met a guru who said to him, "Don't you see how you are poisoning your soul with this success-oriented way of life? Your idea of happiness is to stay up all night studying for an exam so you can get a better grade than your best friend. Your idea of a good marriage is not to find the woman who will make you whole, but to win the girl that everyone else wants. That's not how people are supposed to live. Give it up; come join us in an atmosphere where we all share and love each other." The young man had completed four years at a competitive high school to get into Stanford, plus two years of pre-med courses at the university. He was ripe for this sort of approach. He called his parents from Tokyo and told them he would not be coming home. He was dropping out of school to live in an ashram.

Six months later, his parents got a letter from him: "Dear Mom and Dad, I know you weren't happy with the decision I made last summer, but I want to tell you how happy it has made me. For the first time in my life, I am at peace. Here there is no competing, no hustling, no trying to get ahead of anyone else. Here we are all equal, and we all share. This way of life is so much in harmony with the inner essence of my soul that in only six months I've become the number two disciple in the entire ashram, and I think I can be number one by June!"

This competitive mentality, teaching us to see other people as objects or as obstacles, compounds our loneliness. Slater writes of our constantly dealing with strangers. In fact, the reality may be even worse. We go around all day feeling we are dealing with enemies.

Because we don't know the salesman, the repairman, the woman behind the counter, we suspect that they are trying to cheat us, to take advantage of us. We have been trained to ask ourselves about any offer, "What's the catch? What is he trying to put over on me?" All of our interactions with other people are colored by this mistrust, this suspicion that they are using the encounter to get ahead of us (even as the salesperson may suspect us of taking up his or her time, while planning all along to buy the same item at a discount store). No wonder we find our contacts with other people so exhausting and unsatisfying.

We might think of it this way: if you are running a marathon just to see if you can do it, if you can will your body to run twenty-six miles, you will enjoy the experience. Your legs will ache and your feet will be blistered, but you will have the sense of taking part in an adventure, and the other runners will be your comrades in that adventure, sharing an exhilarating experience that most people will never know. But as soon as it becomes important for you to win that race, it is not fun anymore. Now it becomes a grim, competitive business, and now the other runners are your rivals, no longer your comrades. The result: the loneliness of the long-distance runner.

Kipling wrote: "Down to Gehenna or up to the throne, / He travels the fastest who travels alone." In other words, if your goal in life is to move faster and finish ahead of everybody else, you will find it easier to do that if you're not saddled with permanent commitments, responsibilities for other people in your life. If you have to worry about a husband or wife, children, elderly parents, they may distract you just enough to let someone else get to the finish line ahead of you. Can you think of a more effective attitude for creating a nation full of lonely people?

At the least, loneliness makes life unpleasant and frustrating. At its worst, it leaves us wondering what's the point of living when we are so desperately alone. What can we do, and what role, if any, can religion play in helping us? I would reiterate two important points:

(1) The purpose of religion is not to explain God or to please God, but to help us meet some of our most basic human needs.

(2) Religion helps us not by changing the facts, but by teaching us new ways of looking at those facts.

It makes an immense difference whether we see ourselves as isolated individuals at war with the rest of the world, or as links in a network of human beings working for each other's happiness as well as our own and depending on other people to help us find what we cannot get for ourselves. On this question, the teaching of religion is clear: "It is not good that man should be alone" (Genesis 2:18). In the Bible, God creates the world of nature by separating, introducing divisions and distinctions: "And God *separated* the light from the darkness" (Genesis 1:4); "And God made the firmament and *separated* the waters which were under the firmament from the waters which were above the firmament" (Genesis 1:7). God creates trees, birds, fish, and animals each after its own kind. But when he brings forth human beings, we read: "The rib [or "side"] which the Lord God had taken from man He made into a woman *and brought her to the man* . . . and they became one flesh" (Genesis 1:22, 24).

At the heart of Martin Buber's theology is his concept of the I-Thou relationship. It is a little hard to understand (and the term is clearer in German, French, or Hebrew than in English), but let me try to explain it.

There are two ways of relating to the people in our lives. We can see them as *objects;* that is, they serve a function for us, we get something from them (I buy a newspaper from a vendor), but we are not concerned with how they feel about the transaction. They are only objects for our use. In Buber's terminology we see them as "it." Or we can relate to them as *subjects* ("thou"), letting ourselves be aware that they have feelings about what is happening even as we do.

Many years ago, in an eleventh-grade English class, I read a short story about the wife of a British colonel in India who was expecting important guests for tea one afternoon. She looked out from her front porch after lunch and was horrified to see that the man who swept the leaves off her stairs every morning had not shown up for work. When he finally arrived, she tore into him. "Don't you realize what you've done to me? Do you know who is coming here in an hour? I ought to fire you and see to it that you never get another job anywhere in the city!" Without looking up, the man quietly said, "I'm sorry. My little girl died during the night, and we had to bury her today." For the first time, the colonel's wife was made to see this man not simply as a device for getting her stairs swept but as a human being with a world of needs, pain, relationships to which she had never given thought. Suddenly, he had become a subject, a "thou," a possessor of feelings, rather than an object.

Adolescents, who can be so touchingly idealistic at one moment, skipping meals to raise money for the hungry, running a car wash to help the church youth program, can also be indescribably cruel to each other when they are so wrapped up in pursuing their own ends that they cannot recognize the needs of others. Boyfriends and girlfriends use each other — for sex, for status — and drop each other when they have used the other up. Love is measured by "what I get from him/her" rather than by how much more caring they become in each other's presence. The danger is not only that we will leave people scarred and mistrustful because of the way we treat them, but that we will learn to see all our relationships in exploitative terms, and condemn ourselves to a permanent pattern of detachment and loneliness as a result. Who suffers more, the woman looking for love who is seduced and abandoned by a Don Juan, or the Don Juan himself, who goes through life looking for true love and never permitting himself to find it?

And I suspect we can all recall elderly people we have met who, in their desperate struggle against loneliness, make the chronicle of who has and has not telephoned them the only subject of their conversation. Desperately afraid of being alone, they will grab hold of anyone within reach, telling them the same story they told yesterday, not realizing that they are driving people away with their intense neediness. This is the terrible paradox of loneliness: the more it forces us to focus on our own needs, the harder it becomes for us to be alert to the needs of others, until we become our own worst enemies, chasing people away with our unrelenting focus on ourselves.

It is Buber's contention that we all want I-Thou relationships, that we need that sort of human connection just as we need food, water, and sunlight, but we don't know how to achieve it. We have been too well trained to *use* people rather than to *love* them. His answer is a theological one. God relates to each of us in an I-Thou fashion. God never uses us to meet His needs. He is always aware of our needs and feelings. And by the same token, our relationship to God, if we get it right, will always be an I-Thou relationship. False religion may try to teach us to use God, to push His buttons so that He will give us what we want, to bribe Him with pious actions and flattering words. But such religion only makes God into an object, a God who exists so that we can use Him. True religion, says Buber, teaches us to meet God, not to manipulate Him.

The shallow believer says, "If I pray properly, I will persuade God to make me rich and handsome." The true believer says, "If I pray properly, I will come to know God, and then being rich and handsome won't be nearly as important to me anymore."

God will not use us as objects, and He will not permit Himself to be used by us. (A colleague of mine tells of being asked by a congregant who had just been arrested for embezzlement, "Where is God now that I need Him? Why have I been going to services every week if He won't get me out of the trouble the one time I ask Him to?" My friend gently tried to tell him that he should have been attending services to learn not to embezzle, or to gain the strength not to despair of life and his future when he was caught.) If we achieve a true relationship with God, it will always be an I-Thou relationship in which each participant is as aware of the other as he (He) is of himself. True religion offers to redeem us from loneliness, not by answering our prayers and sending us the man or woman of our dreams, but by teaching us to see our neighbors as ourselves, to be aware of their humanity, their fears and feelings, instead of only being aware of our own. True religion teaches us not how to *win* friends but how to *be* a friend, to be concerned with alleviating the loneliness of others, learning to hear their cry instead of wondering why no one hears ours. When we have learned those lessons, connecting with other people around us becomes much easier.

In one of the great paradoxes at the heart of all religion and all life, when we worry about ourselves, when we consult "how to" books on how to make ourselves happier, we guarantee that our deepest needs will continue to go unmet. When we learn to see the people around us as needing love, as being entitled to love, every bit as much as we are, we discover that we cure our loneliness in the act of reaching out to them. And furthermore, true religion teaches us that, once we have met God, we may find ourselves widowed or unmarried, unemployed or unpopular, but even then, God's closeness will protect us from a sense of abandonment and despair.

What does religion offer that we lonely human souls need? In a word, it offers community. Our place of worship offers us a refuge, an island of caring in the midst of a hostile, competitive world. In a society that segregates the old from the young, the rich from the poor, the successful from the struggling, the house of worship represents one place where the barriers fall and we all stand equal before God. It promises to be the one place in society where my gain does not have to mean your loss. The man worshiping next to you in church may be an insurance salesman or the manager of a rival business, but for the hour you spend together he is not trying to sell you anything or get ahead of you.

My teacher Abraham Joshua Heschel once wrote, "Six days a week, we wrestle with the world, wringing profit from the earth. On the Sabbath, we especially care for the seed of eternity planted in the soul. Six days a week, we seek to dominate the world. On the seventh day, we try to dominate the self. The world may have our hands, but our soul belongs to Someone Else." It is under the auspices of religion, and almost nowhere else in our lives, that we can meet people as brothers and sisters, not as buyers and sellers.

Do you remember Durkheim's findings about primitive religion? He concluded that the purpose of religion in its earliest manifestations was not so much to bring people to God as to bring people together, to protect them from having to see the world as a lonely, hostile place. In times of famine or flood, war or earthquake, people find comfort in facing the danger together. (As I write these lines, farmers in the American Midwest are suffering from a record drought. Like the natives of the South Sea Islands, they are gathering to pray for rain. I am not sure whether they really believe that their prayers will affect the weather, but I know that they draw comfort from the shared experience, the knowledge that their hopes and fears are echoed by hundreds of others like them.) When a child is born, when a daughter marries, when a husband dies, our joy is increased or our sorrow eased when it is shared with others. There is perhaps nothing sadder than experiencing intense joy or intense grief and having no one to share it with.

Can you remember a time in your life when something very good (a marriage proposal, the birth of a child) or something sad (a death or crippling accident) happened? Wasn't your first impulse to call someone up, to tell about it? I remember the day the space shuttle *Challenger* blew up. I was sitting in the public library of my town, and strangers came up to me to tell me about it, because the news was more than they could bear by themselves. They needed to share it. Marriage ceremonies, funerals, and mourning customs are all ways religion gives us of taking a private event and giving it a public expression, so that we are not left alone on those emotional mountain peaks.

This is my problem with the Sunday morning televangelists. It's not just that I disagree with their theology (which I do, but there is plenty of room for all of us). I disagree with their privatizing of religion, making it a matter of the individual's relationship with God rather than calling the individual to become part of a worshiping, celebrating community. And that is why I feel there is something lacking in the life of a person who says, "I believe strongly in God; I don't need a building or a formal service to find Him." Religion is community. It is the way people learn to relate to each other and to belong to each other in truly human ways. Professor Stanley Hauerwas, who teaches ethics at Duke University, has written that when a retarded child is born, the religious question we should ask is not "Why does God permit mental retardation in His world?" but "What sort of community should we become so that mental retardation need not be a barrier to a child's enjoying a gratifying life?"

I remember officiating at the funeral of the twenty-five-year-old son of a friend of mine. The boy's parents were divorced; the relationship with their son, often a stormy one, had just begun to improve when he was killed in a traffic accident. During the forty-eight hours between the accident and the funeral, my friend was inconsolable. His worst nightmare had come true—that he would say goodbye to his son, tell him to drive carefully, and a half-hour later get a phone call from the police telling him the boy had been killed. In the thirty minutes before the funeral service began, he sat in the front row of the chapel, alone at one end of the row, his ex-wife alone at the other end. Friends and neighbors began to come by, to sit with each of them for a moment, to hug them, to hold their hands, to offer a word of sympathy or share a tear. Some fifty or sixty people must have come by in those moments, and with every hug, every tear, I could see his spirits lift a degree. None of us could bring his son back, but we could give him the next best thing, the assurance that he was not left alone in his grief.

The word "religion" comes from the same Latin root as the word "ligament." It means "to bind." As Durkheim discovered, what it does best is bind us to the people around us. Religion is not only a set of statements about God. Religion is also the community, the family through which we learn what it means to be human, and by which we are reinforced in our efforts to do what we believe is right. Religion puts our joys and our sorrows into a context. The birth of our children, the death of our parents are not just statistics. They serve as ways of strengthening or diminishing the community through which we make our lives matter. To the state, the birth or death of an individual means one taxpayer more or less. If ten leave and ten more arrive, there has been no change. But in the eyes of religion, the birth or death of an individual is a unique event, making the community different, adding or subtracting an individual with whom we have a personal, irreplaceable I-Thou relationship.

A few years ago, parents and religious leaders were on the verge of panic as a result of the ostensible success of the Rev. Sun Myung Moon's Unification Church in attracting young people. Bright young college students were being "seduced" into leaving home

and family to devote body and soul to the Unification
Church. We read lurid stories of brainwashings, fund-
raising schemes, and mass arranged marriages, and
wondered what sort of Moon magic was making our
young people act so bizarrely. The answer, it turned
out, was fairly simple. The Unification Church offered
acceptance and community. Faced with an outside
world that was constantly judging and rejecting ("My
father is always after me to improve my grades so I can
get a better job and make more money," "My phone
never rings because I don't have the kind of figure that
boys notice"), the tight-knit community where people
always smiled and "love-bombed" each other was
understandably attractive. (Remember the college student who fled Stanford for the ashram to escape the
materialism and competitiveness of his world?) Instead
of asking, "How could intelligent people fall for that
stuff?" we might well ask, "Why shouldn't young people hungry for love and human connection choose a
community of acceptance and belonging rather than a
world of competitiveness and achievement, a world
with ten losers for every winner?" Or better still, we
might ask, "What was lacking in our churches and synagogues that sent our young people so far afield in their
search for community, for people who would love and
accept them, rather than judge them?"

Our churches betray their mandate, the summons to
create community, when they permit the competitiveness, the success-and-achievement orientation of the
outside world, to infect them. In the ancient Temple of
Jerusalem, when people worshiped God with animal

sacrifices, it was a rule that the animal br
altar had to be perfect. It could not b
crippled. But what of the person who br
fice? Was he expected to be perfect, unblemished? On
the contrary, it was assumed that he was flawed and
imperfect, and was bringing his offering as a way of
transcending his flaws. So the author of Psalm 51 can
say, "My sacrifice, O God, is a broken spirit; a broken
and contrite heart, O God, You will not reject (Psalm
51:29). In other words, he is saying, "If I brought You a
sheep with a broken leg, You would reject me for serv-
ing You with my leftovers, giving You what I could not
sell to the butcher. But when I bring You myself,
bruised and broken as I am, You do not reject me.
Whatever the rest of the world may say about me when
they see me in my fallen estate, I know I am welcome in
Your house."

About a year ago, I found myself sitting across from a
woman in her late thirties who had grown up in our
community before I had come there, had moved away,
and now had returned home for a family occasion. She
told me that she had come to know me through my
books, and that when she was growing up, she rejected
the synagogue because she felt that the synagogue had
rejected her family. Her parents were working people,
barely able to pay their bills and not in a position to
dress well or make a large donation, and she felt that,
though they were good, honest, hardworking people,
they were never taken seriously for that reason. I told
her that I could not comment on things that had happened before I had come to town, but if her parents felt

they were looked down on because they didn't have money, it wasn't the synagogue; it was life. People are like that, I told her. They are impressed by financial success, and thus see the person who is unsuccessful at making money as being a failure in life. If anything, I told her, the synagogue should be the one place in the community where people who can't write a check can gain prominence for their piety, their reliability, their willingness to volunteer and work hard. I have seen it happen time after time: the church and synagogue fashion communities where people are either welcomed without being evaluated or are evaluated by standards much more humane and less materialistic than those of the outside world. In a world in which competitiveness and economic warfare leave us lonely and vulnerable, it should be with feelings of relief that we turn to religious institutions as a safe harbor, a place where no one is trying to get the edge on anyone else, because we all recognize that we are standing together as children of God.

Our churches betray their mandate to fashion community and cure loneliness if they convey an atmosphere of judgment to those who enter. To my mind, it is blasphemous for a church or synagogue to worry about physical comfort—the heat, the lights, the seats, the sound system—but not to realize that a divorced woman who comes to worship is made to feel uncomfortable because some members disapprove of divorce.

Ernest Troeltsch, a sociologist of religion, distinguishes between "church" and "sect." A church is open to everyone. As a result, newcomers feel welcome but members don't always feel close to one another, because of the ease of coming and going. You can never be sure who is seriously involved. A sect, on the other hand, is closed, mistrustful of the world. Only people who know the password are welcome. As a result, people inside feel very close, but are estranged from the rest of humanity outside. Strangers, if admitted at all, are seen as interlopers rather than as prospective members. Our challenge in a mobile, individualistic, competitive society is to recapture the closeness of the sect without its exclusivity.

One of the reasons we find ourselves in the predicament we do, a world full of unconnected people all searching for community, is that we have "desacralized" so many of the things which used to add this dimension of religious bonding to our lives. We have taken things which used to be rich in religious meaning and made them ordinary, leaving us to wonder why there is so little magic in our lives. My favorite example (and one of my favorite activities) concerns eating.

Because of the emotional and biological importance of food, sharing a meal used to be considered a significantly intimate event. Two people who had broken bread together would never think of themselves as strangers again (just as two teenagers on a date sipping the same ice cream soda through two straws realize that they are doing something a little bit intimate). We may or may not accept the Freudian theory that a group of people who kill an animal feel guilty about having shed its blood, and all eat a part of it as a way of distributing the guilt. But we can understand that bringing a sacrifice and sharing it under religious auspices was more than a way of fending off hunger. It was a way of making the participants feel that they were linked to each other by the shared meal. Christians will recognize the significance of communion, a symbolic shared meal derived from the Last Supper which Jesus shared with his disciples, as a way of linking them not only to God but to their fellow communicants. (Note the relationship between the words "communion" and "community.")

Chapter 19 of the Book of Leviticus is known as the Holiness Code. It contains some of the loftiest ethical teaching in all of Scripture, commanding us to honor our parents and the elderly, to be honest in business dealings, to be sensitive to the physically handicapped. Leviticus 19:18 is the original source of the commandment "You shall love your neighbor as yourself." In the midst of these ethical instructions, we find a strange passage telling us that when one brings an animal offering to the Temple, all the meat has to be eaten the same day or on the next day. It would be a very serious infraction to eat any of it on the third day (Leviticus 19:5–8). The usual interpretation is that in a hot climate such as the Middle East, meat spoiled rapidly and it would be unhealthy to eat it forty-eight hours after cooking it. But there are two problems with that interpretation. First, do you really have to pass a law, especially such a strongly worded law, telling people not to eat spoiled food? Can't you depend on people to figure that out for themselves? And secondly, what would such a health regulation be doing in a chapter of ethical instruction?

I would like to offer another interpretation. If a man

brought an animal offering to the Temple (the offering in question is technically known as *shlamim,* an offering of well-being brought in celebration of some happy event) and knew that it had to be totally consumed in two days, what would he do? Rather than waste the meat, he would invite more of his relatives and neighbors. He would share some of it with the poor, the beggars waiting on the Temple grounds hoping for such an invitation. More people would be brought together to share the meal, creating a greater sense of kinship and celebration.

But we today have "desacralized" the act of eating. We have robbed it of its specialness. We eat so many of our meals with strangers, in cafeterias, restaurants, from street vendors, that the intimacy of a shared meal has been lost. Mealtime becomes like time in an elevator; there are other people around but we are expected to pretend we're not aware of them. Families rarely eat together, and when they do, there is seldom a sense of community, of an important shared experience. Eating has become a mundane matter of refueling our bodies the way we gas up our cars. (A fast-food establishment in my neighborhood has a sign in front — PARKING LIMIT 15 MINUTES — as a way of ensuring that meals are consumed promptly and efficiently without becoming social occasions.)

If we could reestablish the shared meal as a religious event which gives people who are strangers to each other the sense of sharing something important, and therefore no longer being strangers, if we could expand the symbolic communion from a ritual to the actual sharing of a meal at the Lord's table, if we could expand the traditional synagogue *kiddush* after services from a cookie nibbled before going home to the actual experience of dining together, we would help reestablish that sense of community which has traditionally been the church's or synagogue's most effective cure for loneliness. If we could renew the tradition of the family gathering for a Sabbath meal or Sunday dinner, we would ease much of the pain of feeling alone in the world.

Organized religion deals with our epidemic of loneliness not by telling us that if we pray properly, God will send us a lover, and not by giving us one more spare-time activity through which we can keep busy and make friends. Rather, it offers us a vision of a world where people no longer condemn themselves to loneliness by seeing all other people as rivals. It offers us a place to which we can bring our whole selves, not just that part of ourselves that we bring to our jobs and our hobbies, and to encounter the whole selves of our neighbors in a way we cannot meet them anywhere else. And it offers us the opportunity to share in worship. My professional responsibility to conduct services gives me the opportunity to see what an effective worship service can do. When it works (and I have presided over a lot of services that did not work), its effect is truly magical. People enter as separate individuals, troubled, lonely, not sure if they are in the right place, and the experience of shared worship transforms them. When liturgy works, it becomes more than a matter of proclaiming the right words and being strengthened by them. We all recite the same words in prayer, not because we all believe the same things (how could we?), but because in the process of reading together, singing together, chanting together, something truly remarkable happens. We transcend our sense of being unconnected individuals. We are lifted out of our individual isolation and transformed into a single organism, singing and rejoicing in the presence of God.

"THEY WILL MOUNT UP WITH WINGS AS EAGLES"

A WOMAN WHO SIGNS HERSELF "FOREVER Guilty" recently wrote to Ann Landers:

Six years ago, on New Year's Eve, my husband John and I went to a party at the home of friends. We were in the mood to celebrate. After five years of scrimping and saving, we had bought a modest house and repaid in full our college loans. John had one more semester of law school and excellent job prospects. So we were really in the mood to live it up.

John and I are not drinkers but that night there was a lot of champagne around and we had several glasses. Everyone was having a wonderful time and the party didn't break up until dawn. Actually saying good night to the host was the last thing either of us remembers until after the accident. God forgive us, we ended the life of a 13-year-old boy who was delivering bakery goods on his bicycle. Witnesses said he was dragged more than 200 feet. The doctors did everything they could to save him but his injuries were too extensive. The lad never regained consciousness and died after four days.

In those few moments when we got the news, the entire world changed. Never again will it be the same. That little boy who was the light of his parents' life will never grow up, fall in love and be a source of pride to his family and a contributing member of society. Why? Because he happened to be in the wrong place at the wrong time.

We called on the family but they refused to see us. Who could blame them? The day of the funeral we sent roses and sat in the back row of the church. When we came home, we found rose petals and broken stems scattered over our front steps.

My husband never finished law school. He lost his job (couldn't concentrate) and was unemployed for several months. He was impotent for almost a year. I ate compulsively and gained 40 pounds. Neither of us slept much. There were recurring nightmares. . . .

Intensive therapy and support from family and some friends kept us going. People kept saying, "Life goes on." It does if they mean the sun comes up every day, but the kind of existence we had could hardly be called living. I must keep writing before I lose my courage. Maybe this letter will make an impression on someone. It only takes one drink for some drivers to become involved in a tragedy like ours. If you don't hurt, maim or kill yourself or a loved one, you might kill a little boy who is trying to earn some extra pocket money.

We have no way of knowing from the letter how the parents of the boy who was struck down have fared in the six intervening years, whether or not religion was helpful to them in coping with their loss. As one who lost a fourteen-year-old son, not to accident but to illness, I can say that in the twelve years since his death, I have not known a day in which I did not think about him, in which I did not probe the empty space his death left behind like a tongue probing a missing tooth. But I know, too, that religion has given me the strength to bear his loss without being broken by it, to remember but to be able to enjoy life.

But what about the other family, the law student and his wife who caused the accident and six years later wrote the letter? Must they remain "forever guilty"? There is no changing the result of the accident that cost the life of an innocent child, but does it have to darken their lives perpetually as well? Too often in my career as a rabbi I have officiated at the funeral of an innocent person struck down by a drunk driver, and I have urged society to crack down on drunk drivers, to make them recognize and bear the consequences of what they do. But if I were asked to bring religious consolation not to the victim's family but to the driver and his family, what would I have to say?

Some years ago, our local community hospital added a chapel where people could sit and meditate in the midst of the stress that is so frequently a part of the hospital scene and for religious services for ambulatory patients and for doctors and nurses who had to work on Sundays and holidays. I had been on the planning committee, and was invited to speak at the dedication. I spoke of the uses to which the chapel would be put, of the extra dimension it added to the hospital routine. At the reception that followed, a young doctor took me aside and said, "Rabbi, I enjoyed your remarks, but there is one thing the chapel promises to do that you're probably not aware of because you're not a physician. It answers the question: Where does a doctor go when he feels he has made a mistake?

"Sometimes, looking back on a case, I get the feeling I should have done things differently. I'm not talking about a major ethical or diagnostic blunder, faulty treatment or anything like that. Just a vague sense that I don't feel good about the way I handled something. Maybe I should have spent more time on it, been more concerned with the emotional impact of the illness on the patient as well as the physical impact. I know I have the tendency a lot of us doctors have, when we have bad news to share, to deliver it in technical language and then leave the room before the family really understands what has just hit them. Maybe I should have consulted with colleagues who have seen more cases like this than I have, but I didn't feel like taking the time.

"Where do I go with feelings like those? I can't share them with the patient and his family. I'd lose their confidence and possibly open myself up to a malpractice lawsuit. I can't tell my superior about it. I'm afraid it would reflect on my evaluations and future career. I hate to bring it home and dump it on my wife. She doesn't understand these things. All she can say is 'I'm sure what you did wasn't that terrible,' and that just doesn't help. I get to feeling terribly guilty and depressed. But when I heard you talking about the chapel, it occurred to me that if I could go there and talk to God, tell Him what I had done and how I felt about it, I would feel better."

"Forever Guilty" and her husband did all the right things, the things I recommend to people who have done something they feel guilty about. They went for therapy. They turned to their support network of family and friends. And it helped to some degree. They felt sustained, but they did not feel forgiven. Human beings can't grant that sort of existential forgiveness; only God can forgive. Even if the parents of the boy had accepted their flowers, invited them into their home, and told them they understood it was all an unfortunate accident (probably a superhumanly unrealistic expectation), I suspect they still would have borne the guilt of what they had done. There are some things we cannot do for ourselves, and we cannot even do for each other. Removing the burden of guilt is one of them. Neither therapy nor human assurance and acceptance can do that. We need God to wash us clean.

In the Book of Psalms, there are two great poems articulating the human need for forgiveness. One of them, which I will discuss shortly, is Psalm 51. The other is Psalm 32:

Happy is he whose transgression is forgiven, whose sin
  is covered over.
Happy is the man whom the Lord does not hold guilty,
And in whose spirit there is no deceit.
As long as I said nothing, my limbs wasted away

From my anguished roaring all day long.
For night and day Your hand lay heavy on me.
My vigor waned as in the summer drought.
Then I acknowledged my sin to You,
I did not cover up my guilt.
I resolved "I will confess my transgression to the Lord,"
And You forgave the guilt of my sin. [Psalm 32:1–5]

There are two reasons why we find it hard to shed the burden of guilt when we have done something wrong. The first is that we make ourselves feel so vulnerable when we admit our imperfections. Somewhere along the way, we have picked up the idea that in order to be deserving of love and admiration, we have to be perfect. If we can only manage to be perfect, everyone, even God, will *have* to love us. Admitting any weakness, any mistake, we think, will give people reason to reject us. As a result of this outlook, we have trouble admitting that we are ever wrong. Every alleged mistake on our part has to be explained as someone else's fault. (It reminds me of a bumper sticker I saw: "The man who can smile when things are going badly has just thought of someone to blame it on.")

The sad part is, we never even notice how unpleasant and unbearable we become when we insist we are always right. And the equally sad corollary is that the more we suspect we may in fact have been wrong, the more stubbornly we fight to justify ourselves. So the doctor who feels he should have handled a case differently can't admit it to his patient or to his supervisor. The husband who did something he is embarrassed about can't admit it to his wife. The worker who has made a mistake is afraid to admit it to the boss. They are all afraid that, if they take off their protective armor and admit they were wrong, if they make themselves vulnerable in the name of honest self-disclosure, the other person will take advantage of them and hurt them. We are all afraid to admit our weaknesses, for fear that other people will use them against us. Husbands and wives have hurt each other so often (because they are so vulnerable to each other), employers have fired or punished workers, patients have sued doctors, for honestly admitting a mistake, to the point where we have learned to be afraid of admitting our faults.

As a result, we walk around with a split soul, part of us embarrassed by what another part of us has done. That is why the psalmist writes, "As long as I said nothing, my limbs wasted away." (Buber once wrote, "In telling a lie, the spirit commits treason against itself.") When we add the embarrassment of concealing the truth to the embarrassment of having done wrong to begin with, we come to think of ourselves as pretty rotten people. We start saying to ourselves, "Other people may like and admire me, but that's only because they don't really know me. If they knew the real me, they would think as little of me as I do of myself." And that is a terrible situation to be in. That is why the psalmist finds it such a relief when he can honestly unburden himself to God, and to his astonishment, learns that God does not reject or punish him for his honesty. It is why he begins his Psalm not only by saying "Happy is he whose transgression is forgiven," but by adding a second line, "Happy is the man . . . in whose spirit there is no deceit." In other words, he is saying, "It's wonderful to learn that God still loves me despite what I've done, but it's equally wonderful to know that I don't have to lie and pretend anymore for fear that the truth about me will come out."

Why can we admit our failings to God more readily than to people around us? Because we can be sure God won't use our admission to hurt us. Imagine the following scenario: Beth, a young housewife, has taken a large sum of money, several thousand dollars, out of the family's joint bank account without her husband's knowledge and invested it in a stock a girlfriend assured her was poised to take off. Two weeks later, the stock has fallen to less than half of its original value. What can Beth do? The longer she waits to tell her husband what she did, the more afraid she is of his reaction, and the more ashamed she is of what she did and of not telling him. She finds herself growing distant from her husband, avoiding conversations with him, even as she knows that this will only make things worse when the truth finally comes out.

When she thinks about telling him, she imagines three possible outcomes. He might lose his temper, throw things, yell at her. "You're a thief and a liar! How can I ever trust you again?" Or he might say, "Is that what you've been worried about these last few days? I was afraid it was something worse—an affair, a serious illness. Listen, it's only money. It was an honest mistake; it's not going to send us to the poorhouse. Forget about it; don't let it upset you." (Harry Golden tells the story of losing a five-dollar bill his parents had given him when he was a child during the Depression and spending all day in the park, afraid to go home. When he finally got over his fear and embarrassment and went home, his parents were so relieved to have him home safe that they said, "Better to lose the money than to spend it on doctors.") Or he might say, "You should have told me about it, let me check it out. I know you meant well, you wanted to surprise and impress me, but you really went about it the wrong way. Let's sit down and figure out what we can cut out of our budget to replace what we've lost."

Beth is so frightened of the first possibility, of what it would mean for her marriage and her self-image, that she can't find the courage to tell her husband the truth. But strangely, she is a little afraid of the second response as well. She doesn't want her mistake dismissed. It would make her feel that she was being treated like a child, that her actions were not being taken seriously. This is why a lot of people find that going to a therapist does not relieve them of guilt feelings. They sense that therapists are too ready to say, "That's all right, you meant no harm; lots of people do that," and that is not what they need. In Archibald MacLeish's retelling of the story of Job, one of Job's comforters is a psychiatrist who urges him not to feel guilty. "There is no guilt, my man. We are all victims of our guilt, not guilty." Job replies, "I'd rather suffer every unspeakable suffering God sends, knowing it was I that suffered, I that earned the need to suffer, I that acted, I that chose, than wash my hands with yours in that defiling innocence." We are not helped by being told we should not feel guilty because we are not competent to make a moral choice.

Beth would find it a lot easier to confront her husband with what she did if she knew she could count on getting the third response, in effect: "What you did was wrong, but it doesn't shatter the love relationship between us. I didn't fall in love with you because you were perfect. I fell in love with you because I found your mixture of strengths and weaknesses irresistibly appealing, and I sensed you saw me the same way."

We can turn to God with our guilt, as the author of Psalm 32 did, as the young doctor who spoke to me at the chapel dedication felt he could, because we can count on His love. God does not expect us to be perfect; He knows us too well. How did we ever think we could fool Him into believing we were perfect by not telling Him all the facts? I know there are some prominent clergymen—I hear them on the radio and see them on television from time to time—who tell us that God will reject us and consign us to eternal damnation if we sin even once (I have to wonder what kind of parents they grew up with). But I don't believe that. God loves us enough to forgive our mistakes and at the same time He loves us enough to take them seriously, to ask us to do something to make up for them.

I said earlier that there are two reasons that make it hard for us to shed the burden of guilt we feel for the wrong things we have done. One is our fear of vulnerability—that other people will take advantage of our confession to hurt us. The second reason is that wrongdoing erodes our self-image. We may make a mistake once, but for a long time afterward we carry in our heads the sense of ourselves as someone who made that mistake. We are likely to think of ourselves as weak, selfish people because of it.

It seems that the human mind works in some ways like a computer (or is it the computer that works like a human mind?). Many computer programs have what is known as "feedback" built into them. When a certain situation is responded to in a certain way, the computer "learns" from that and remembers it the next time the situation comes up. Our minds seem to operate similarly. If we once respond to an uncomfortable situation by lying, if we once pad our expense account, if we once cheat on our diet by snacking when no one can see us, we have not only done something wrong once. We have taught ourselves, by a kind of "feedback" process, to respond to that temptation the next time by saying to ourselves, "I am a weak person who handles temptation by giving in." Each time we repeat the behavior, we reinforce that message.

Think of it this way. You are standing at an intersection, not sure which way to go. At that moment, it seems equally convenient to take either path. Once you make your choice, every step you take, the farther you continue down that road, means it will be that much harder, to turn back and take the other one, even if you begin to suspect that you have made a mistake.

Guilt is so insidious because it teaches us to say not only, "I told a lie" or "I took something that didn't belong to me," but "I am a person who lies [or steals]." That is no longer just a statement about a specific act in the past; it has been generalized to encompass the present and future.

I had never known Judy. I had met her parents through shared community activity, and I knew the rabbi of the congregation to which they belonged. It was he who told me her story. As a teenager, Judy had gotten caught up in the craziness of the early seventies. A bright girl, she had started experimenting with drugs in her junior year in high school. She dropped out of college midway through her freshman year and drifted into a life of drugs and sex. Her distraught parents heard from her only when she needed money, and when they stopped sending it to her, she broke off all contact. They had no way of knowing where she was living, or even if she was still alive.

Then one morning, Judy woke up in a shabby apartment, in the bed of a man she didn't even like, and said to herself, "I don't want to live like this anymore." She went home. Her parents welcomed their prodigal daughter with the proverbial fatted calf. The first thing Judy did was take a long hot bath and wash her hair, not just for relaxation and hygiene, but as a symbolic washing away of the sordid past she was leaving behind. Instinctively, without realizing why, she felt she needed to immerse her body as a symbolic rebirth to a newer, cleaner sense of herself. Next, she told her parents, she wanted to go to temple. She felt she had messed up her life and had to find her way back to God. Overjoyed at their daughter's return to their life, they took her to services at their local Conservative temple on Saturday morning. It was a disaster. There was a bar mitzvah ceremony for a thirteen-year-old boy, and the congregation was filled with his relatives who sat there fidgeting and looking at their watches through the two-hour service. The sermon was about the need to be vigilant against a possible resurgence of anti-Semitism. Judy never heard the name of God invoked once during the entire morning. A week later, she left home again and became part of a small community of evangelical Christians.

I think I understand what happened to Judy. When she broke with the sordid life she had been leading, she felt degraded. That was why the first two things she needed to do were to take a bath and go to synagogue. She needed to break with her past and feel acceptable again. I suspect Judy was afraid of two things when she called to tell her parents she was on her way home: either that they (and all of respectable society with them) would reject her, slamming the door in her face (remember Beth's first imagined outcome), or they would not take her sin and self-degradation as seriously as she herself took it (Beth's husband's second possible response). Judy felt she had done some truly shameful things. To be told "It's all in the past; there were a lot of mixed-up kids in those years" would have meant that her parents could not understand or accept the powerful feelings of shame and contamination that Judy had brought home with her.

Human forgiveness often comes too cheaply and easily. That is why Judy needed God. He seemed to be the only one who would recognize the depravity to which she had sunk and would accept her anyway. And that is why the synagogue service, with its middle-class banalities, was such a disappointment. Not that another synagogue, or the average mainline Christian church, would necessarily have been better. I suspect that our "respectable" middle-class suburban religious institutions of whatever affiliation don't have the vocabulary for meeting the religious and emotional needs of the person who feels fallen and worthless, and needs to hear the message, "God sees how contemptible you have made your life, and He is prepared to lift you out of the mud, wipe away your filth and embrace you as His own." You can't talk like that to your average suburban churchgoer. And yet people like Judy need precisely that message: not "What you did doesn't matter; I love you anyway," but "What you did matters grievously, and I forgive you for it." That is why Judy had to join an evangelical sect (where, by the way, she remained for two years and then came home again).

My readings and personal contacts with born-again Christians and Jewish *baalei-teshuva* ("those who return") make me believe that many of them turn to God against a background of self-disgust — drugs, alcoholism, sexual promiscuity, a life of lying and fraud. What they need is a sense of radical forgiveness that will simultaneously recognize the sinfulness of what they have done and affirm them as people worth caring about. That may be what the author of Psalm 32 had in mind when he praised God, not for forgiving his sin, but for forgiving "the *guilt* of my sin," the sense the original deed had left him with, that he was not worthy of being loved.

I think of the many passages in the Psalms where a person had to hit bottom before he experienced God's cleansing and forgiveness:

Out of the depths I called to You, O Lord . . .
Yours is the power to forgive. [Psalm 130:1, 4]

Purge me with hyssop and I shall be clean; wash me and I shall be whiter than snow. [Psalm 51:7]

I think of the "twelve-step" process pioneered by Alcoholics Anonymous and used by so many other groups to help people break addictive habits and regain their sense of self-worth. Alcoholics are asked to admit they are alcoholics, and to turn to a Higher Power to do for them what they are not able to do for themselves. As long as people tell them, "Take charge of your own life," as long as well-meaning relatives conspire with them to avoid facing the seriousness of their situation, as long as they feel that they can handle their problem themselves without outside help, they will never be helped.

To go back to the question we began with many pages ago, if "Forever Guilty" and her husband, still haunted by the memory of having caused the death of a thirteen-year-old boy, were to turn to me for help instead of to therapists or to Ann Landers, what would I say to them?

I might begin by recognizing the seriousness of what

they had done. Unlike many people I see who feel guilty, they truly had something to feel guilty about. Through their negligence and carelessness, an innocent child was killed. There is no minimizing the seriousness of that. But then I might make the theological distinction between sin as an event and sin as a condition. That is, "You did something very wrong, but that doesn't make you a chronic wrongdoer." There is a difference between the person who does wrong once and the person for whom it becomes a lifestyle. The person who steals once, under pressure of temptation or economic hardship, is different from the person who steals for a living or as a way of getting back at society. The question, I might say to the law student and his wife, is not whether you did a terrible thing six years ago. You did. The question is whether that one event should define your characters. Let's talk about the other kinds of things you do, or might start doing, not to erase the tragedy of the past but to balance it.

In ancient Israel, a person who felt he had done something wrong would bring to the Temple a special kind of animal sacrifice known as the sin-offering. It was not meant to undo the past. It was not a bribe to persuade God to erase the record of his sin. It was intended to help the person see himself in a different, more favorable light. He could now say to himself, "Sometimes, I admit it, I am weak and selfish. But look, sometimes I can be strong and generous too. Sometimes I am embarrassed by what I do, but not always. Sometimes I have reasons to feel good about myself."

I would say to "Forever Guilty" and her husband, "If

there were anything you could do, however painful or expensive, to bring that boy back to life, I know you would do it. But there isn't. So let's talk instead about what you can do to bring your self-respect back to life. What can you do to enable you to say, 'Sometimes we're weak and careless, but sometimes we're strong and noble and generous'? Can you contribute time and money to Mothers Against Drunk Driving? Can you go back and finish law school, and spend a third of your time on public service work, on being a lawyer for the poor and the handicapped? Not as a penance, you understand, but as a way of letting your good, decent, noble side emerge from under the shadow of that New Year's Day tragedy?"

And finally, I would tell them to turn to God, to ask whether God sees them as "forever guilty" or whether He sees their good, clean, caring side as clearly as He sees their weak, careless one. And can they learn to see themselves as God sees them?

I visited a man in the hospital recently who had lung cancer. He had been a two-pack-a-day smoker. His wife and children had pleaded with him for years to give it up, but he would laugh and tell them that he would rather live a short life with beer and cigarettes than a long life without them. He wasn't laughing now. He was frightened, and he felt guilty about what he had done to himself, and what he would be doing to his family. What could I say to a man in his predicament? I couldn't say what I often say to people in hospital beds, "Look, it's not your fault; this is not a punishment for anything you did. You're a good person who doesn't deserve this." He feels he does deserve it, and it *is* a punishment (or at least a consequence) of the way he lived.

Instead, I said to him, "I know you are feeling very bad now, not only because you're seriously ill but because you're telling yourself you did this to yourself. This didn't have to happen if you hadn't been so stubbornly addicted to cigarettes. Well, let me tell you something. I believe in a God who loves even people who mess up their lives the way you did, even people who mess up their lives a lot worse than you did. I've come here to sit at your bedside as an embodiment of that message of God's love. You may be down on yourself right now, but you deserve to know that you are cared about by a whole lot of people. Your wife and children aren't angry at you for being sick. If they come across that way, it's because they love you so much and they're afraid for you and for themselves now that you're sick.

"Can you believe that the doctors and nurses are going to work hard to help you, not because you're paying them or your insurance company is paying them, but because God is guiding them to become people who care deeply about every fellow human being who is ill? Can you believe that friends and family and your rabbi will come to visit you and try to cheer you up, though it's hard for us to see you in pain, because we feel that's something you need and deserve from us? You may be down on yourself, but a lot of people you care about care very much about you in return. The doctors will do all they can to help you, but even the best of doctors can fall short. You'll have to help yourself get better, and I hope the knowledge that God and I and your family are on your side will make it easier for you to do that."

The other great poem of God's forgiveness is Psalm 51, which tradition ascribes to King David after he recognized the wrongness of his adultery with Bathsheba:

Have mercy upon me, O God, as befits Your faithfulness;
In keeping with Your abundant compassion, blot out my transgressions.
Wash me thoroughly of my iniquity, and purify me of my sin,
For I recognize my transgression and am ever conscious of my sin. . . .
Purge me with hyssop till I am pure,
Wash me till I am whiter than snow. . . .
Fashion a pure heart for me, O God,
Create in me a steadfast spirit.
Do not cast me out of Your presence,
Or take Your holy spirit from me.
Let me again rejoice in Your help,
Let a vigorous spirit sustain me.
Let me teach transgressors Your ways
That sinners may return to You.
  [Psalm 51:3–5, 9, 12–15]

Where Psalm 32 emphasized the writer's need to confess his faults and still be accepted, this Psalm (which also includes the verse "God, You will not despise a contrite and broken heart") adds another dimension. Beyond the assurance of God's love and acceptance, it asks for God's help. Its author is saying, "There are some things I can't do for myself, and making myself feel good and clean again is one of them. Weak and imperfect as I am, I can't make myself feel clean. I need Your help." So he writes, "Purge me with hyssop till I am pure, wash me till I am whiter than snow," referring of course to his internal, not external, defilement. "Fashion a pure heart for me, O God." He can't single-handedly bring about a change of heart any more than the alcoholic or the compulsive eater can change his habits by an act of will. We all need God's help to give us the strength to do that which we find it hard to do alone.

People who do wrong things to themselves or to others *should* feel guilty for what they have done. They would be psychopaths, moral monsters, if they did not. If their guilt moves them to do good, to balance the bad, if it makes them more careful, more caring, it will have been constructive guilt. But no one should be condemned to feel "forever guilty." How do we rid ourselves of the stain of guilt after we have paid our debt to society for it? We can't. We can't rid *ourselves* of guilt, because guilt is rooted in our perception of how other people see us. We can invite God to lift the stain of guilt from our souls, because He demands honesty from us but not perfection, and because He and He alone has the power to give us a transfusion of moral strength we could never get by our own efforts (we know, because we have tried). God can do for us what we cannot do for ourselves. As the sages of the Talmud put it, "There is no happier person in all Jerusalem than the one who has brought a sin-offering to God's altar and leaves the Temple feeling forgiven."

But redemption from the burden of sin and guilt is only one of the things God does for us which we cannot do for ourselves. What about those of us who don't feel perpetually guilty, who have never struck a pedestrian while driving drunk, who have never ruined our health or betrayed our marriages? Where do we need God? Let me tell you a personal story:

In June 1981, I told my family that my goal for that summer was to get into shape to run the Falmouth Road Race, a seven-mile mini-marathon which takes place every August in Falmouth, on Cape Cod. They were very supportive, and to help me get into shape to run seven miles, my daughter Ariel bought me a T-shirt on the back of which she had printed ISAIAH 40:31. If you look it up, you will see that the verse reads, "Those who trust in the Lord will have their strength renewed. They will mount up with wings as eagles. They will run and not grow weary." It didn't make me a champion at Falmouth, but that verse has been very important to me ever since. It teaches me where to find God in this unpredictable and often discouraging world. God is the Power that replenishes, that renews our strength when we have used up all our strength.

I can believe in the reality of God, despite the things that have happened in my family and in the families of people I care about, because I have seen Him work miracles. Not like the miracles of the Bible, suspensions of natural law, splitting the sea, bringing the dead back to life—God works miracles today by enabling ordinary people to do extraordinary things.

Somewhere in the oncology ward of a hospital, a child is dying of leukemia. Her parents are at her side, praying for a miracle. Friends and relatives, all the members of their church or synagogue are praying for a miracle. But she dies, just as the doctors feared she would. Was there no miracle? Were their prayers mocked? Sometimes the miracle is not that the child survives. The miracle is that the parents' marriage survives, despite the awful strain that the death of a child places on a marriage. The miracle is that the parents are prepared to go on affirming life and risking the vulnerability of loving each other, even after they have been so badly hurt by life. The miracle is that the faith of the community survives, that they are able to go on believing in the world and the value of prayer, even when they have learned that this is a world where innocent children die. I have seen miracles like that happen (some of them have happened to me). I have seen weak people become strong, timid people become brave, selfish people become generous. I have seen people care for their elderly parents, for brain-damaged children, for wives in wheelchairs, for years, even decades, and I have asked myself, Where do people get the strength to keep doing that for so long? Where do they get the resources of love and loyalty to keep going? The only answer I come up with is the one Ariel printed on my T-shirt eight years ago, that when we are weary and out of strength, we turn to God and He renews our strength, so that we can run and not grow weary, so that we can walk and not feel faint.

This is perhaps the most significant difference between me and a morally committed atheist. We are both good people, honest, helpful, generous. We both work for world peace and racial harmony. We both strive to make our communities better places to live. What difference, if any, does religious commitment make? The difference comes, I think, when we have exhausted ourselves in caring for the hurt and the grieving, when we have fought the demons of injustice and bigotry for years and yet they are just as strong as when we started. What do we do then? Where do we turn for the strength to go on working and fighting, when we are at the point of running out of strength? How do we go on giving, when we have been giving for so long and have nothing left to give? The atheist, for all that he is a good person, a model citizen, believes that strength and love come from within himself. So he looks deep into himself for more strength, and may well find that he has at last run dry. I have the advantage of believing in a God who is beyond myself, a God who renews my strength when I turn to Him, who replenishes my capacity to love, to care, to work, who gives me strength so that I can go forth again and share my strength with others.

The prophet Jeremiah put it this way: "Cursed is he [a better translation would be "Alas for him"] who trusts in man, who makes mere flesh his strength and turns his thoughts from God. He shall be like a bush in the desert, set in the scorched places of the wilderness. Blessed is he who trusts in the Lord. He shall be like a tree planted by waters, sending forth its roots by a stream. It does not sense the coming of heat, its leaves are ever fresh" (Jeremiah 17:5–3).

What is the difference between a person who relies only on himself and a person who has learned to turn to God for help? Not that one will do bad things while the other will do good things. The self-reliant atheist may be a fine, upstanding person. The difference is, the atheist is like "a bush in the desert." If he has only himself to rely on, then when he exhausts his internal resources, he runs the risk of running dry and withering. But the man or woman who turns to God is like a tree planted by a stream. What they share with the world is replenished from a source beyond themselves, so that they never run dry.

I am often asked to speak to medical staffs, hospice workers, and other caregivers about how to deal with victims of tragedy and misfortune. I always spend the last few minutes of my talk dealing with the problem of "caregiver burnout," that sense of emotional exhaustion which causes teachers, social workers, and even doctors and nurses to stop giving to those in need because "it takes so much out of me." I suggest that burnout is not the result of hard work but of a sense of futility. People can work hard for long hours if they feel that they are making a difference. But if they feel that their efforts are being wasted, that no matter how hard they work it won't make any difference, then any task becomes too hard.

Do you remember the story from the Book of Exodus of how Moses was carrying the tablets of the Law down from Mount Sinai, and when he saw the Israelites worshiping the Golden Calf he threw the tablets to the ground and broke them? There is a Jewish legend about how that happened. Moses was already an old man at the time. Climbing down a mountain while carrying two large stone tablets must have been difficult for him. But because the tablets were engraved with God's words, he found the strength to do it. He felt he was doing something important. But when Moses saw the Israelites dancing around the Golden Calf, the legend tells us, the writing disappeared from the tablets, and they became just two heavy stones. At that point, Moses could no longer hold them, and they fell from his hands and broke. When Moses realized that the people were not going to live by God's laws, he no longer had the strength to do what he had been able to do before.

I tell doctors and other caregivers that the first thing they have to do to avoid that sense of futility is to redefine success. Success may not mean that the patient survives the operation or walks out with her problem solved. Some illnesses will be incurable, some problems insolvable. Instead, I tell them, success should mean giving every patient, every client, the feeling that he or she is cared about, no matter how desperate the situation.

I met a clergyman once who told me that he had recently conducted a healing service for AIDS. Suspicious that he was one of those miracle-working television hucksters, I said to him, "I didn't know you

AIDS by prayer." He answered, "Of course
...re AIDS by prayer. That's not what I try to
heal families, to bring reconciliation between
the AIDS patient and his often embarrassed, often
angry parents, between the patient and his former lover
who has moved away and doesn't return phone calls,
and most important, to heal his relationship with himself and with God. I understand that my prayers can't
keep him from dying, but they may be able to keep him
from feeling condemned and abandoned as he faces
death."

And then I tell the caregivers: You are in a profes-
sion that calls on you to give to others, to care for people, to feel their pain and their anger, and to do this
you have to have a religious commitment. You need
the resources of a religious faith. Otherwise you will
run dry. If you spend your love and your strength and
your compassion on others, and you have no Source
from which to replenish it, then one day you will find
yourself depleted of love and depleted of strength.
You will start to resent people for bringing you their
problems. You will end up short-changing your family, and you will find your job more than you can
handle. If you have no source of strength other than
yourself, you will end up like Jeremiah's desert
plant.

But if you learn to turn to God to refill what you use
up, if you let yourself become the channel through
which God's love and caring flow on their way to help
others, then your strength will be continually renewed.

❈   ❈   ❈

There will be times in our lives when we need help, because we won't be able to do for ourselves what we desperately need done. When we are financially bankrupt, we cannot lend ourselves the money to solve our problems; we need help from beyond ourselves. In the same way, when we feel guilty and inadequate, we cannot forgive ourselves. Forgiveness has to come from a higher source. And when we feel exhausted from the effort to be a good, caring person, from helping build a better world, we cannot renew our own strength. We cannot supply ourselves with the one thing we are out of. For that, we have to turn to God to renew our strength so that we can keep running and not grow weary.

7

CAN MODERN PEOPLE PRAY?

SISTER REJEANNE KELLEY, A ROMAN CATH-
olic nun, tells of the home in which she was raised: "My
mother had a vigil light and a statue of St. Anthony. When
she didn't get what she wanted, she would blow out the
light and turn St. Anthony to the wall. When she got what
she wanted, back he'd come and she'd light the candle
again."

Some years ago, the papers carried the story of a man
in Florida who sued his minister. It seems the man had
been in church one Sunday when the minister gave a
sermon based on the Scriptural passage "Cast thy bread
upon the waters." He urged the congregation to be
charitable and generous, telling them that God would
reward them tenfold. The man subsequently made a
large contribution to the church, and when his business
did not prosper, sued the minister for false preaching.
(The case was thrown out of court and the man was
told to take sermons less literally. I wonder if the
preacher argued in his own defense that giving money

in order to be richly compensated was not charity but calculated investment.)

We tend to think that for religion to work, for our prayers to be answered, we should get what we ask for. That is to say, we have confused God with Santa Claus. We think that prayer means giving God the list of things we want and assuring Him that we have been good girls and boys and deserve to get them, and if we haven't been good, the rules we broke were silly rules anyway.

When we pray sincerely and intensely for something—the child praying to find a bicycle under the Christmas tree, the teenage girl praying for someone to find her attractive and love her, the adult praying for the survival and return to health of a loved one—when we shower God with pleas and promises and still don't get what we prayed for, we are left wondering what went wrong. Is there something wrong with us? Were our prayers not fervent enough, our promised changes not enough of a sacrifice? Are we not good enough people for God to heed our prayers?

Or is there something wrong with God, that He is not moved by our desperate plight and honest pleading? Why won't He give us what He seems so ready to give other, apparently less deserving people? Or maybe there is something wrong with religion itself. Maybe there is no God who hears prayers. Maybe our pouring out our hearts, our fears, our promises to change, end up in some celestial dead-letter office, "Addressee Unknown."

Sometimes the same thing happens when we attend

church or synagogue, looking for a religious experience, looking for something spiritual to happen. Perhaps we are confused, perhaps we are spiritually hungry and lonely. We are not sure exactly what it is we are looking for, but we vaguely sense that the church or temple is the place to look for it, and that we will recognize it when we see it. An hour or two later, we walk out with the same feeling we have after seeing a mediocre movie. We find ourselves evaluating the sermon, the choir, the friendliness of the ushers, and deciding that all of them were well intentioned, but something, the one thing we went there looking for, was missing.

We wonder if the fault is in ourselves, that we never learned to appreciate religion any more than we learned to appreciate modern art. Are we perhaps spiritually tone-deaf? Or was it religion that is at fault? Perhaps it is a case of "the emperor's new clothes," where everyone really finds religion boring and irrelevant but is too polite or hypocritical to admit it.

I don't think any of these reactions is valid. There is nothing wrong with religion if we would only understand it properly, and neither is there anything so terrible about most of us that God should withhold from us the rewards of religion and prayer. What happens most of the time is that we are disappointed in religion because we are doing it wrong.

Too often, we try to use religion as a way of controlling and manipulating God. We think that if we say the right words or perform the right actions, we can get God to do what we want Him to. If we stopped to think about it, we might wonder how an awesomely powerful, all-wise God could be controlled by a few words from the likes of us. But after all, we might reason, a three-ton automobile can be made to do what we want with the pressure of our fingertips. The fearful power of electricity can be tamed to do our bidding. Computers are so much faster and more efficient at handling information than we are, but once we know how to operate them, we can make them do all sorts of things. And perhaps we remember how, when we were children, our parents were much more powerful than we were, but we mastered the art of persuading them to give us what we wanted from them because they loved us. So what is so unreasonable about attempting to control God?

Quite simply, God will not suffer Himself to be manipulated by our words or deeds. That is not religion. A century ago, Sir James Frazer, in *The Golden Bough*, suggested that this was the difference between religion and magic. Religion, he said, is the attempt to serve God. Magic is the effort to manipulate God. When we turn to religion as a way of getting God to give us what we want—be it health, love, riches, or whatever—we run the risk of being disappointed, not because we are unworthy of being loved or being rich, and not because God is stubborn or spiteful or incapable of helping us, but because that is not what religion does.

Prayer is not a matter of coming to God with our wish list and pleading with Him to give us what we ask for. Prayer is first and foremost the experience of being in the presence of God. Whether or not we have our requests granted, whether or not we get anything to take home as a result of the encounter, we are changed by having come into the presence of God. A person who has spent an hour or two in the presence of God will be a different person for some time afterward.

I am told that the Eskimos have more than a dozen words for snow because snow is an important part of their environment. They find it useful to distinguish between falling snow, frozen snow, melted snow, and all its other forms. For us, snow is only an occasional inconvenience (I write these lines shortly after having shoveled it off the front walk of my Massachusetts home), so we make do with one word to cover all of its manifestations.

If prayer were an important part of our lives, instead of an occasional diversion, we would probably have many words for it. Instead, we stretch the same word to refer to a public reading of a prescribed liturgy at a prescribed time, to the desperate wish of a terminally ill woman, to the spontaneous gasp of delight and awe we feel when we see the sun on the mountain or the spring flowers or the stars on a clear night. Those are all prayers, those are all encounters with God, but they are very different spiritual experiences.

In congregational worship, regularly scheduled services on a Saturday or Sunday morning, I have come to believe that the congregating is more important than the words we speak. Something miraculous happens when people come together seeking the presence of God. The miracle is that we so often find it. Somehow the whole becomes more than the sum of its parts. A spirit is created in our midst which none of us brought there. In

 us came there looking for it because we did
 it when we were alone. But in our coming
 er, we created the mood and the moment in which
 is present.

The psalmist says, "Lord, I love Your Temple abode,
the dwelling place of Your presence" [Psalm 26:8]. But
on an average Tuesday or Wednesday morning, the
sanctuary of my synagogue stands darks and empty. I
am not sure it can be described as "the dwelling place of
[God's] presence." Only when people enter it in a mood
of reverence and spiritual search does it become a house
of worship.

We don't go to church or synagogue at a stipulated
time because God keeps "office hours." We go because
that is when we know there will be other people there,
seeking the same kind of encounter we are seeking.
That is why it makes sense to read words someone else
has written, words that may or may not reflect what we
believe. The purpose of reading those words is not to
fool God into thinking we share the pious sentiments of
the prayer's author. The purpose is for us to join in song
and prayer with our fellow worshipers, to find God in
the exhilarating experience of transcending our isolation, our individuality, and becoming part of a greater
whole. When the service works, we will feel different
about ourselves and the world for having gone through
that experience.

But why does a congregational prayer service sometimes not work? Party because miracles don't always
happen when we schedule them, but partly too because
even if the clergy and the choir and the ushers know

their parts cold, we may not have learned ours.
in thinking of ourselves as an audience, with the same
anticipation we bring to a visit to the theater. "A good
movie can reach me emotionally; let's see if a good religious service can do the same." (Sometimes the archi-
tecture of the house of prayer conspires to make us
think that way. It invites us to sit back and watch the
professionals perform.) But we can't be passive spectators if we want to experience the magic of worship.
Without our active participation, it will not happen.

Sometimes services fall flat because we have lost the
art of listening. We think prayer involves talking to
God, persuading him, telling Him things He would not
otherwise know. We may realize that millions of other
people are bringing their cases before God, but we
think that if we increase the intensity and fervor of our
prayers, then, like the correspondent who shouts loud-
est at a White House press conference, our cry will
catch God's ear. We need to be reminded that prayer
involves listening perhaps even more than speaking. It
involves opening ourselves to what God wants *us* to
hear, in a setting purified of the noise and distractions of
the everyday world.

When communication between a husband and wife
breaks down so that they are no longer sharing with
each other, the rift can take one of two forms. Either
they can stop talking to each other entirely and sit
walled off in silence, or they can fill the air between
them with static, meaningless noise, verbal busywork,
to hide the fact that they have nothing to say to each
other. ("Please pass the vegetables." "What time do we

have to pick up the kids?" "What's on television tonight?") When we lack the art of communicating with God, when we don't know how to talk to Him and don't know how to listen, we can show that either by keeping out of His way or by filling the channels with empty verbiage, pious-sounding words that never engage our hearts, as a way of trying to camouflage the fact that we don't know what to say to Him and don't believe He has anything to say to us.

If God is not Santa Claus and prayer is not primarily a matter of telling God what we would like Him to do to make us happy, what does prayer accomplish? For one thing, if we have learned to listen while we pray, prayer can remind us of things we would probably not be thinking of otherwise. Prayer can remind us to be grateful. Prayers of thanks for the food we eat remind us not to take it for granted. They serve not only to remind us of people going hungry, but of the miracle that occurs when seeds and soil, rain and sun combine to produce our daily sustenance. They remind us of the chain of people involved in producing, processing, packaging, and distributing the food that ends up on our tables.

The first five minutes of a Jewish daily morning service contain blessings in which I thank God for the fact that:

My mind works and I know it is morning,
My eyes work,
My arms and legs function,

My spinal column works and I can stand upright,
I have clothes to wear,
I have things to look forward to during the day.

Without these prescribed blessings, it might not
occur to me to be grateful for all of those things. I might
have to wait until I encountered a blind man or a crip-
ple, and then my gratitude would be mixed with a large
dose of pity.

Gratitude does not come naturally to most people.
We tend to assume that we are entitled to all the good
things in life just for being the nice people we are. We
have to be taught to be grateful. ("Say thank-you to
Grandpa for the present, and don't let him hear you
complain that it's so small." "Did you write all the
thank-you notes for your graduation presents?"
"Honey, would you mind finishing writing the thank-
you's for the wedding gifts? I find it a chore.")

There is a Hassidic story about the tailor who comes
to his rabbi and says, "I have a problem with my
prayers. If someone comes to me and says, 'Mendel,
you're a wonderful tailor,' that makes me feel good. I
feel appreciated. I can go on feeling good for a whole
week, even longer, on the strength of one compliment
like that. But if people came to me every day, one after
another, hour after hour, and kept saying to me,
'Mendel, you're a wonderful tailor,' 'Mendel, you're a
wonderful tailor,' over and over again, it would drive
me crazy. It would soon get to the point where I
wouldn't want to listen to them anymore. I would tell
them to go away and let me do my work in peace. This

is what bothers me about prayer. It seems to me that if we told God how wonderful He was once a week, even once every few weeks, and just one or two of us at a time, that's all He would need. Is God so insecure that He needs us praising him every day? Three times a day, morning, noon, and night? Hundreds of people praising him? It seems to me it would drive Him crazy."

The rabbi smiled and said, "Mendel, you're absolutely right. You have no idea how hard it is for God to listen to all of our praises, hour after hour, day after day. But God knows how important it is for us to utter that praise, so in His great love for us, He tolerates all of our prayers."

God does not need our flattery, but we need to become the sort of people who know how to be grateful. Look at what we have done to Thanksgiving. We have made it a day on which we complain about having eaten too much, and then turn our attention to the football game, because we are so uncomfortable sustaining a sense of gratitude for more than a moment.

I once read an essay by a man who had formed the habit of writing "thank you" in the lower left-hand corner of all his checks as he paid his bills. He would write a check to the electric utility or the phone company, and as he penned in the words "thank you" in the corner, he would think of all the ways in which his life was made more comfortable by the fact that the company regularly and reliably provided him with its services. He would write a check to the bank for his monthly mortgage payment and pause for a moment to reflect on the comfort of having a roof over his head. He would pay his water bill and as he wrote "thank you" in the corner, he would say to himself that the water wasn't all that great-tasting and probably had some chemicals in it that were bad for him, but how long ago was it that his fore-bears had to pump water from the well in winter and worry about its going dry in summer. Even when he was not all that happy about writing a check, as when he paid his income tax in April, he disciplined himself to write "thank you" on the check, not because he believed that the IRS computer would notice it and be gratified, but because it was his way of reminding himself that he should feel grateful to be living in this country and enjoying the benefits that American democracy pro-vides.

Once we get over the Santa Claus mentality, prayer can be that kind of discipline, not an inventory of what we lack but a series of reminders of what we have, and what we might so easily take for granted and forget to be grateful for.

A man who has just been interviewed for a good job stops off at a church on the way home and prays that he gets the job. A woman visiting her husband in the coro-nary care unit of a hospital stops off at the hospital chapel to pray for his recovery. Do we really want to think of God as a God who has the power to grant those wishes, and chooses to give us or deny us what we pray for? Will praying affect either the employer's decision or the patient's recovery? Do we want to measure the usefulness of prayer on the basis of whether the man gets the job or not, whether the husband survives his heart attack or dies? I have religious friends who like to say, "God always answers our prayers, but sometimes the answer is no." I confess I don't like that outlook. It not only implies that God knows what is good for us better than we ourselves do, but that we should not weep or feel bad when things turn out wrong for us, because God wanted it to happen that way. That outlook leads us to believe that God could control everything for our benefit, that He could send us health and prosperity, if we could only find the right words and the right level of fervor to make Him want to.

Some people say God does not grant our prayers because people's prayers are mutually exclusive. Farmers pray for rain and families with picnics scheduled pray for sunshine. One group of fans prays for the home team to win, while another prays for the visitors. God can answer one set of prayers only by denying the other. I would rather believe that rain is caused by meteorological factors, and that ball games are won by a combination of skill and luck, without God's intervening to arrange the outcome.

Does that mean that the man is wasting his time when he enters the church, or the woman when she steps into the hospital chapel? I think not. I think they gain two things from their prayers, even if they don't get what they are praying for. First, they gain the reassuring knowledge that they are not alone. God is with them in their fear and uncertainty, to help make an uncertain future that much less frightening. The man and the woman are turning to God in prayer in part because they feel they have lost control over their own lives. Things are affecting their lives in which they have little say. They feel alone and helpless. How might God answer their prayers? He might say to the woman in the hospital chapel, "I can't guarantee that your husband will survive this crisis. If I could, no one would ever die because every patient has someone who prays fervently for his recovery. But I can assure you that you are not so alone as you may feel you are. Friends are calling you, people are praying for you, offering to help you. It may well help your husband's chances to know that so many people are rooting for him to pull through. And when you do feel alone and frightened, know that you can always talk to Me, a God who stands for life and healing."

And He might say to the man on his way home from the job search, "I hear your prayer, your fears and hopes. I can't arrange for you to get the job. That's not My role. But I can tell you this. I cherish all of My children, no matter how well or poorly they do in the business world. My way of measuring success has nothing to do with the amount of your salary, the size of your office, or the impressiveness of your job description. And the members of your family, the people who matter the most to you, see you the same way. For Me, that person is successful who has learned how to love, to share, and to master his impulses. I can't give you a job, but I can help you gain a sense of humility if you get the job, and the gift of resiliency and self-respect if you don't, with the reassurance that I am near and I think well of you in either event."

Second, prayer is a coming to terms with our limitations. That may be one reason why so many people find it hard to pray today. In this modern age, we are not accustomed to accepting limits. We are more likely to have been raised with the attitude "You can do anything you want if you put your mind to it and work hard enough at it." If that adage is meant to urge us to make the most of our abilities, it is probably true. But at the same time it is also false and misleading. I will never be a professional athlete, a ballet dancer, a surgeon, or a poet no matter how much I put my mind to it. It is both cruel and unfair to set me up to blame myself by implying that, if I didn't accomplish something, it was my own fault for not trying hard enough.

When I pray for health, when I pray for world peace, when I pray for the capacity to see other people in a favorable light, one of the things I am doing is acknowledging that there is much that I want and need which I cannot get by my own efforts. I am not so much asking God to give me those things as I am admitting that I cannot attain them without His help. I can probably make myself sick by my own efforts, if I eat, drink, or smoke too much or don't dress warmly in cold weather. But no matter how much I exercise and watch my diet, I can't make myself healthy. I need something beyond my own power—call it luck, call it grace—for that. I can make myself obnoxious and unlovable without outside help. I can make other people dislike me. But no matter how rich, smart, or good-looking I may be, and no matter how many books I read on the subject, I can't make someone love me. To ask God for these things is not to order items from a heavenly catalog, but to overcome the illusion of self-sufficiency and confess my dependence.

When do I pray? I try to pray during Sabbath services, but sometimes the responsibility of conducting the service makes that hard. I try to maintain a discipline of personal prayer, but the flesh is weak and the distractions are many. I am most likely to pray in my study, when I have a schedule of counseling appointments. My secretary buzzes me to tell me that my next appointment has arrived—someone with a marital conflict, a problem with a rebellious child, a recent widow who can't get over her depression—and I say to myself, "This person is coming to see me because she has a problem she can't handle. What makes her think I can help her? I'm not necessarily any wiser than she is." In those moments between receiving the call and opening the door to let the person in, I pray. I pray that I will be worthy of the expectations and the confidence the person is reposing in me. I pray that she will not be disappointed in the value of religion because she does not feel helped by the time she spends with me. I pray that God will grant me the insight and the inspiration to help this person, that He grant me the patience to hear her story without judging her, that He make me a channel for His love and His strength, to share it with those of His children who are in need.

I think we can all learn to pray that way, trusting that when we reach the borders of our own strength and cunning, God will take us by the hand and lead us, unafraid, into new and uncharted territory.

Dr. Gershon Rosenstein, a prominent Russian scientist, a specialist in the chemistry of the brain, discovered religion as an adult and prevailed on the Soviet government to let him go to Israel, where he could practice his newly claimed faith. Shortly after his arrival there, he was interviewed about how a scientist could suddenly accept religion. He said among other things, "I remember the first time I tried to pray, to probe the depths of my heart and reach God. My scientific mind said to me, 'You fool, what are you doing? To whom do you think you are speaking?' To this day, I have a great fear about what would have happened to me if I had not overcome my intellectual hesitations at that moment."

What would have happened to him? He would have spent the rest of his life stuck in the illusion of self-sufficiency, believing that his own strength and intelligence were all he had, and all he would need, to make it through life. In another Hassidic story, the disciple comes to the rabbi and says, "I have a terrible problem. I can't pray. I try to say the words but nothing happens. I don't feel anything. What should I do?" The rabbi answers, "Pray for the ability to pray."

Psalm 73 is a spiritual masterpiece, a favorite of many people who know the Book of Psalms well. It is the account of a man who found himself doubting God because of the world's unfairness and found his answer not in theology but in the experience of God's presence:

God is truly good to Israel,
To those whose heart is pure.
As for me, my feet had almost strayed,
My steps were nearly led off course,
For I envied the profligate,

I saw the wicked at ease. . . .

[I thought to myself] It was for nothing that I kept my
  heart pure

And washed my hands in innocence,

Seeing that I have been constantly afflicted,

That each morning brings new torments.

Had I decided to say those things,

I should have been false to the circle of Your disciples.

So I applied myself to try to understand this,

But it seemed a hopeless task

Till I entered Your sanctuary. . . .

You held my right hand,

You guided me by Your counsels

And led me toward honor.

Whom else have I in heaven?

And having You, I want no one on earth.

My mind and my body may fail,

But God is the Rock of my mind, my portion forever.

Those who keep far from You perish . . .

But as for me, nearness to God is my good.

  [Psalm 73:1–3,13–17, 23–27]

The author of that deeply moving Psalm begins with
an experience many of us have. He sees selfish, wicked
people prospering. He sees good things happening to
bad people and he wonders, "Was it for nothing that I
kept my heart pure?" Are religion and morality just a
fraud designed to keep us docile while the wicked take
advantage of us? He finds no answer to his question "till
I entered [God's] sanctuary." And then, the answer is
not an explanation. The answer is the experience of the

nearness of God, the experience of feeling that God is taking him by the hand. In the light of that experience, all doubt, all philosophical and intellectual questions melt away. As Martin Buber points out in his commentary on Psalm 73, God answers his questions not by explaining the apparent prosperity of the wicked, but by making him one of the pure of heart. There is still evil in the world and it is still our obligation to oppose it, to expose and punish the wicked. *But once we have tasted the presence of God, we will no longer envy the wicked.*

What do we get from prayer, if it will not help us choose a winning lottery ticket or achieve a miraculous recovery from illness? We get a sense of being in God's presence, and that can put both our victories and our tragedies in a different perspective.

If we live every moment of our lives in the secular world, we will come to define success and happiness in secular terms. The world will be a battlefield, a constant struggle for advancement and advantage, dividing us into winners and losers. If we pray at all, our prayers will be prayers for victory: "God, give me a place among the winners."

But if we learn the art of entering into God's presence, we will learn to see success and happiness in other, more human terms. Our prayer will not be "Give me this because I deserve it" or "Give me this because I need it." Our prayer will not be the prayer of the jealous child competing for his share of parental love, "Do for me what You have done for others, so I will know that You love me." Our prayer will be the prayer of the author of Psalm 73, asking for nothing but humbly giving thanks. "As for me, nearness to God is my good."

FOR THOU ART WITH ME

The Lord is my shepherd; I shall not want.
He makes me lie down in green pastures,
He leads me beside the still waters,
He restores my soul.
He guides me in straight paths for His name's sake.
Yea, though I walk through the valley of the shadow of
    death,
I will fear no evil, for Thou art with me.
Thy rod and Thy staff, they comfort me.
Thou preparest a meal before me in the presence of my
    enemies.
Thou anointest my head with oil; my cup runneth over.
Surely goodness and mercy shall follow me all the days of
    my life,
And I shall dwell in the house of the Lord forever.
    [Psalm 23]

THERE IS PERHAPS NO CHAPTER IN ALL THE Bible as beloved as Psalm 23. It may well be the only chapter of the Bible that millions of people know by heart. One commentator writes that "it has dried many tears and supplied the mold into which many hearts have poured their peaceful faith." But let me point out something in the Psalm that you may never have noticed before, however often you may have read it.

You remember Martin Buber's concept, explained earlier in the book, of the difference between I-It and I-Thou relationships. We can either talk *about* other people, relating to them as objects, thinking only of how they can be useful to us. Or we can talk *to* them, being aware of their presence, their feelings, seeing them as subjects in their own right. Now let us look again at the familiar Psalm 23, this time asking ourselves: When is the psalmist talking *about* God as an object ("He"), and when he is talking *to* God as a real presence in his life ("Thou")? (Buber defines religion as experiencing God,

and theology as talking about God, and goes on to say
that the difference between religion and theology is the
difference between having dinner and reading a menu.)
When is the Psalm being theological, and when is it
being religious?

He makes me lie down in green pastures,
He leads me beside the still waters,
He restores my soul.
He guides me in straight paths for His name's sake.
Yea, though I walk through the valley of the shadow
    of death,
I will fear no evil, for *Thou* art with me.

We are often told that in times of prosperity people are
ready to affirm God, but as soon as something bad happens to them they collapse in despair and conclude,
"There is no God." The author of Psalm 23 tells us that, in
fact, the opposite is true. When things are going smoothly
for us, he says, when we find ourselves in green pastures,
God remains something abstract. God is "He," the remote
Creator that keeps the world going. We believe in God
the way we believe in the existence of the South Pole or
the validity of the Pythagorean theorem. But when things
go badly, when we find ourselves walking in the valley of
the shadow of death, that is when God becomes real. No
longer an abstract "He," God is now "Thou": "I could
never have made it through this time were it not for You."

It is in our fear of death that we Americans betray the
fact that we are not a religious people. If we could let

ourselves believe that our souls were immortal, death would not frighten us, because death would not mean obliteration of our essential self. Because of our fear of death, we worship youth. We fawn over professional athletes, even over college and high school football stars, because we cherish the attributes of youth more than the wisdom of age. We envy young people for being so much further from death than we are. (Actually, except for being able to run fast and drink coffee late at night, there are few advantages to being young.) We are uncomfortable in the presence of the elderly, resenting their demands on us, segregating them in retirement communities and nursing homes, because when they are around, they remind us of our own vulnerability to decline, to aging and ultimately to death. We are uneasy with the bereaved, the crippled, the terminally ill, because their situations force us to confront the subject we are least comfortable talking about. (Studies repeatedly show that doctors, nurses, and relatives spend less time with dying patients than they do with patients who are on their way to recovery. Widows report that their situation makes even their closest friends uncomfortable.) At a certain point, we might begin to lie about our age, dye our hair, and think seriously about cosmetic surgery. We turn to diet and exercise as though, if we can just get our cholesterol count low enough, we could cheat death and live forever.

We are afraid of dying, we cling to life so desperately, not because we enjoy living so much but because we are afraid that this life is all there is. When it is over, it will be truly over. All trace of our existence will disappear. We go to all sorts of extremes to avoid the prospect of disappearing totally after death. I am not talking about the handful of people who have their bodies frozen to wait for a medical breakthrough, nor do I have in mind those whose religion promises them that the faithful will be taken alive to heaven and never have to die. (A friend of mine who sells insurance told me of meeting such a person, who wanted his life insurance rewritten to provide for his family not only in the event of his death, but also in the event of his bodily assumption to heaven, leaving his wife and children, who belonged to a different denomination, behind.)

I have in mind rather the people who give large sums of money to colleges, museums, or hospitals to have their names permanently inscribed on buildings. If you can afford that, it is one way to achieve immortality. The world-renowned scientist who has trained two generations of grateful students but still feels that his life is incomplete because he has never won the Nobel Prize is after the same kind of assurance that, even though he will not live forever, his name will, if only in textbooks and encyclopedias. The philosopher Bertrand Russell told of once having had a nightmare in which he saw a librarian holding his book *Principia Mathematica* and trying to decide whether to leave it on the shelf or discard it to make room for more recent books. What was at stake in that dream was nothing less than his immortality, the question of whether future generations would know his name and continue to study his ideas. (Isn't it interesting how much we are concerned with our *name* living on after us, as if that somehow symbolized our essential self. I wonder if that is why men have historically been more gratified by the birth of a son than of a daughter, since the son would carry on the family name.)

The author of Psalm 23 understood that it is not death that people find frightening; it is "the shadow of death," the knowledge, which no other animal lives with, that one day we will die. Over the centuries, religion has tried to deal with that fear by promising us immortality in a World to Come. There, we are told, we and our loved ones will live forever in eternal bliss. There, the last will be first and those who suffered unfairly in this life will be compensated.

I confess I have problems with that promise. First, I have to wonder how much of it is wishful thinking. The fact is, I don't know what happens to us after we die and neither does anyone else. Beyond that, much as I might want to live longer and regain the companionship of people I have loved and lost, an eternity which would be a lot like this life but would never end might be a little hard to take. But I do have a religious belief in the immortality of my soul.

Let me explain what I mean. I have a body, but my body is only part of who I am, and not necessarily the most important part. My body can change, I can gain or lose weight, change my hair style or color, even lose a limb, and I will still be the same person. The real me is found in that part of me which is not physical—my values, my memories, my habits, my personality, my sense of humor. As long as they remain unchanged, I will still be me. Don't we say of a person who looks the same but has begun to behave differently, "She's just not herself these days"? And of the person who has made himself over physically but continues to behave the way he always did, we sigh and say, "Same old Fred."

Some people call that nonphysical part of a person "spirit" or "personality." I am comfortable using the traditional religious word, "soul," to refer to that energy, that combination of propensities, values, and memories that every one of us has, as personal and unique as our fingerprints, as long as we are alive.

When I die, my body will be buried and gradually decay and return to the earth. But what will happen to my soul? I believe that, because it is not physical, a soul cannot die. I can't imagine what happens to it, because my mind can only think in three-dimensional terms and can't conjure with the notion of where nonphysical entities "go" when they no longer have bodies to incarnate them. It is like asking where the light goes when you turn off the switch, or where ideas are stored before anyone thinks of them, or what happens to jokes that nobody tells anymore. There may be answers to those questions, but my mind cannot conceive of them.

I do know, however, that people's souls live on. The lesson survives even after the teacher is no longer with us. When I sit down to write a sermon, I feel the presence of the man who was my rabbi when I was growing up. When I read a book, I bring back to life my high school and college teachers who taught me to appreciate literature. When I try to help someone cope with pain and suffering, I am accompanied and guided by the memory of my late son and the example of how he coped with pain and illness.

In physics, there is the law of conservation of matter and energy (which Einstein taught us are different forms of the same reality). Nothing disappears; it is transformed from one form to another. The dead bird we bury becomes part of the soil that makes the grass grow. When we step on the brakes to slow down the car, the energy is transformed into heat that is sent out into the world. Why should there not be a law of conservation of spiritual energy? Words of comfort, gestures of caring, deeds of charity do not disappear into thin air after they are done. They continue to reverberate. At some point in our lives, we choose either to be truthful or to lie. The moment of decision is over, and we consign it to history. But the law of conservation of energy operates in spiritual matters as relentlessly as it does in physical ones. Our choice of truth or falsehood does not disappear into history. It continues to shape our mental image of ourselves: in a crisis, are we people who face up to truth or try to evade it? It sets an example for our children, and for others who look to us.

Traditional religion offered us the prospect of the World to Come where we would be rewarded for our good deeds and punished for our wicked ones. Because the World to Come was portrayed in geographical terms, with a heaven "up there" and a hell "down there," and we were told we would "go" to heaven or "be sent" to hell, we moderns tend to scoff at the idea. We have explored the universe pretty thoroughly and have located neither heaven nor hell. But suppose we learned to think of the World to Come not in spatial but in temporal terms, as its name actually suggests, not another place but another time. Suppose the truth—comforting to some, terrifying to others—is that the things we say and do are immortal and outlive us. Hell would be the knowledge that our being sarcastic to our daughter will cause her to be sarcastic to our grandchildren, that the lie we so cleverly told in 1985 will cause two people to mistrust each other in 1995. Heaven would mean realizing that our willingness to stand up for an unpopular cause may not have changed things in 1979, when we did it, but without our knowing it, will inspire other people to take similar stands in the year 2000. In the physical world, every time I wave my arm I set the air in motion and the reverberations never stop. In the realm of the spirit, every time I dry a tear, hold someone's hand, cause a student's eyes to light up with understanding, I have set something in motion which will never stop. It will have consequences that I have caused but will never know about.

Would we live differently, would we behave differently and choose differently if we understood that the consequences of what we choose to do will exist forever? Would we push ourselves that much harder to do something right, something generous, which we can't quite get ourselves to do now because we are not sure it really makes a difference? Would we hesitate to do something cruel or dishonest if we knew that its effect would not be limited to the day or week of the deed but would pollute the air around us forever? I would like to think we would. And is it this, not angels with harps and devils with pitchforks, that religion offers us when it speaks of reward and punishment in the World to Come? I would like to think that it is.

If I live to the age at which my father died, my life will soon be two-thirds over. I take a lot of airplane trips and am always aware of how vulnerable planes are to disaster. I officiate at funerals of people my age and younger. I have known death; I have buried my parents and my son. It is time for me to ponder the question of my own mortality.

My religious perspective offers me the assurance that, though my body will one day give out, the essential Me will live on, and if I am concerned with immortality of that sort, I should pay at least as much attention to my soul, my nonphysical self, as I do to my weight and my blood pressure. God cannot redeem me from death, no matter how good a person I am, but He redeems me from the fear of death so that I don't have to clutch frantically at this life as if it were all there is. He lights my path through "the valley of the shadow of death" by assuring me that the words I have written and spoken, the hearts I have touched, the hands I have reached out to, the child I leave behind, will gain me all the immortality I need. More than that, I am assured that even when the last person who ever knew me dies, and the last copy of my book has been removed from the library shelf, the essential me, the nonphysical me, will still live on in the mind of God, where no act of goodness or kindness is ever forgotten.

My religious outlook not only armors me against the fear of total disappearance after death but helps me

cope with the knowledge of my own mortality by defin-
ing what it is that makes my life mean something. The
writer Michael Ignatieff, in a magazine article dis-
cussing books to help us cope with sickness and death
[*The New Republic,* Dec. 26, 1988], writes:

> The modern problem is not the problem of dying without
> religious consolation. The problem is that dying after ill-
> ness can make the whole narrative of selfhood appear
> senseless. One can accept that death is our natural fate . . .
> and still feel in the grip of the metaphor of injustice, the
> conviction that death is unfair because it arrived before we
> have brought any order to the story of our life. Yet if death
> is natural, if it is "without meaning," why should justice
> have anything to do with it? Being run over on the street,
> for a young man of 41 with two kids, a novel half-finished,
> and a whole life to live may be a misfortune, but it is not an
> injustice.

One of the points Ignatieff is making is that death is
tragic and painful only if life is meaningful. Death hurts
only because life is precious, because love is real, and
we see being separated from someone we love by death,
by illness, by human crime as an outrage against God's
plan for the world. Some religions try to teach us that
death and separation are not really painful. It is life that
is painful, and if we resigned ourselves to that fact and
did not want more from life than life is likely to give us,
the death of a loved one, his "graduation" from this
world to a better one, would not hurt. Some nonreligious people similarly try to tell us that death is nat-

ural and inevitable, and therefore it makes no sense to defy it or be hurt or outraged by it. When a lion pounces on a zebra, it is not good and it is not tragic. It is simply dinner. It is nature taking its course. And when a person dies of cancer or is run down by a speeding car, it is neither good nor bad. It is just another instance of nature taking its course. Speaking strictly logically, we should be more upset if the person *survived* the heart attack or the serious automobile accident, because that would mean that the laws of nature were not operating as we usually expect them to.

Why, then, are we outraged by the death of the young, by the terrorist bomb that brings down a passenger plane? Only because we believe, at a level that logic and intellectual reasoning cannot explain, that life *should* be fair, that the life of any individual is too sacred to be ended prematurely or casually. And only the sense that we are living in the sight of God, that every one of us is precious to Him, undergirds that belief.

When I am resting in green pastures, beside the still waters, I may not realize that I need God. But when life becomes turbulent, when I realize how tenuous my grip on life may be as I read of mass disasters or see someone my age die, when I worry that death may come and render meaningless everything I have worked so hard for, that is when I need God. I need to know that "You are with me in the valley of the shadow."

I am intrigued by the fact that the psalmist speaks of "walk[ing] *through* the valley of the shadow of death." As a rabbi, I deal with many people who are coping with bereavement. I see them in the days after the funeral, and I see them in synagogue throughout the first year of mourning. Too often, I see in them a willingness to remain in the shadow, a sense of "I will never be happy again; I don't deserve to be happy." I can understand the psychological mechanism at work here, the guilt, the depression. But I also know how wrong it is, how unhealthy it is, to become one of those creatures who are comfortable only in the dark and gloom, who shrink from bright lights and laughter. The poet Kahlil Gibran writes of people who "stand with their backs to the sun, and what is the sun to them but the caster of shadows?" I want to help them attain the wisdom of the author of Psalm 23, that God will not bring back your loved one, but He can do the next best thing. He can take you by the hand and guide you *through* the valley of the shadow of death until you come out again into the sunlight on the other side. He can bring you to the understanding that loss is painful only because life is good and life is precious. The death of a human being is tragic whereas the death of a barnyard animal is not, precisely because human life has meaning. And human life has meaning not in economic terms (some racehorses and prize bulls are worth more money than some people), not in intellectual terms (retarded and brain-damaged human beings are still human beings), but only in religious terms.

A Christian pastoral worker in Central America, working with insurgents against a repressive government, tells of hearing a woman cry out, "Why is God doing this to us?" and hearing her neighbor answer, "God has abandoned us. If we have not done anything bad, if what we are asking for is not all that much, where is God now?" The pastoral worker had no answer. But it seems to me that there is an answer, and it might be something like this: Where is God when people are tortured and murdered by a tyrannical government? Where was God when a handful of Jews in the Warsaw Ghetto rose in defiance of the Nazi army? Where was God when black people were brutalized by angry mobs and bigoted white sheriffs in the American South? God is found in the courage of the human soul to stand up for human dignity, no matter what the odds, so that no matter how poor, no matter how uneducated or how badly outnumbered, people are willing to risk their lives for what they believe is right. What source, if not God, gives people the power and courage to say, "I may die in the attempt, but I will die one day anyway, so I might as well spend my life in the service of something I believe in." God is not found in happy endings. God is found in the human being's capacity to cherish something as being more valuable than life itself, and in our recognizing that it is precisely that capacity that makes human life precious to begin with.

Where is God when brave people are murdered? The answer might be "God cannot guarantee that you will survive, or even that your side will win sometime soon. He can only promise you this—that if you die, your sacrifice will not have been in vain. Deeds of courage and self-sacrifice are never meaningless. Don't feel that

you are a failure when you lose one battle in the service
of a cause that deserves to win. Even as a match has the
power to light a candle and perpetuate its light before it
is consumed by its own flame, even as a candle can
chase the darkness from an entire room before it uses
itself up in the process of shedding light and warmth, so
your dedication will make a difference to people whose
existence you may not even know about today." Some
problems are too grave to be solved in one lifetime. In
those cases, we need God to link one lifetime to
another, to join one heroic sacrifice to another, until justice triumphs.

The Jewish activist Natan (Anatoly) Sharansky was
imprisoned by the Soviet government on false charges
of spying for the United States and sentenced to fifteen years of hard labor. Despite the efforts of the
Soviet government to break his spirit, he survived his
sentence and came out of prison stronger than he went
in, by constantly reminding himself that the Power he
relied on was greater than the power of those who
kept him in prison. God could not open the doors of
his jail cell, but God could keep him free wherever he
was. When he lit Hanukkah candles in his cell, when
he celebrated Passover by recalling the Exodus of the
Hebrew slaves from Egypt, he reminded himself that
he was freer than his captors. Only his body was in a
Russian prison; his mind, unlike theirs, was not
enslaved. When he was finally released and permitted
to go to Israel, he told his story in an autobiography,
and chose for its title a passage from the Psalm he

would recite to himself when things were hardest, *Fear No Evil.*

A person dies, perhaps painfully, perhaps prematurely, and in our anguish we ask, "Where is God?" Where is God? God is found in the incredible resiliency of the human soul, in our willingness to love though we understand how vulnerable love makes us, in our determination to go on affirming the value of life even when events in the world would seem to teach us that life is cheap. God is found in our insistence on finding our way through the valley of the shadow, knowing that there is evil in the world, knowing that some of the time the evil may overpower us, yet fearing no evil, "for Thou art with me."

WHY IS GOD SO HARD TO FIND?

THERE IS A FAMOUS HASSIDIC STORY ABOUT the sage who came home from the synagogue one day and found his nine-year-old daughter crying bitterly. He asked her what was wrong, and she told him, between sobs, that she and her friends had been playing hide-and-seek and when it was her turn to hide, she hid so well that they had given up on finding her and went off to play another game. She waited and waited for them to find her, and finally after about an hour, had come out to find herself all alone.

As the sage comforted her, he mused to himself, "I wonder if this is how God feels. He threatened that if we abandoned His ways, He would hide His face from us and deprive us of His presence. I wonder if God has managed to hide from us so successfully that we have given up looking for Him and have gone off in other directions. And I wonder if God feels lonely and abandoned."

Why is God so hard to find in the modern world?

How did we get ourselves into this situation where we have problems—loneliness, moral confusion, the pointlessness of so much of our lives, our fear of death—problems to which religion has traditionally provided answers, but it never occurs to us to look to religion for help? Or if we do look, why are we so often disappointed?

I think there are many reasons. One reason is that, while the abstract concepts of religion, prayer, and morality may be of divine origin, the embodiments of organized religion here on earth are human institutions, created and run by fallible human beings, and never quite able to avoid the flaws of their human creators. I may have a wonderful idea, but in the process of trying to explain that idea, to put it into words, it inevitably turns out to be less clear and less wonderful than when it existed, unarticulated, in my mind. And if the playing out of that idea calls for the involvement of other people, then the purity and nobility of the original concept is even more likely to be compromised by the distractions, sensitivities, and ego needs that those people (including myself) bring to the project.

Religion, the search for the presence of God and the difference that presence makes in our lives, is a sublime idea. Churches and synagogues are the result of human efforts to bring that sublime idea down to earth, and are as imperfect as their human creators are. When someone says to me, "I tried to get involved in your synagogue, but I found it to be full of petty, small-minded hypocrites," I can usually resist the temptation to tell him, "That's all right, there's always room for one more." What I say instead is, "A synagogue that admitted only saints would be like a hospital that admitted only healthy people. It would be a lot easier to run, and a more pleasant place to be, but I'm not sure we would be doing the job we are here to do." The people who staff God's embassies on earth are sometimes, but rarely, saints. Most of the time, they are flawed, imperfect, inconsistent, weak, and confused. This is the case, not because churches attract the insecure and problem-ridden, but because most of us are like that to some degree, but the religiously aware are brave enough to see their flaws and try to do something about it.

What about the person who says, "Religion may be fine for those who can't make it without help. I don't need it because I'm strong enough to handle my own problems"? One of the recurrent themes of this book has been the idea that the original sin, the wrong turn from which so many subsequent mistakes and problems follow, is not disobedience or lust, but the arrogant claim of self-sufficiency, the idea that we don't need help, that we are strong enough to do it entirely on our own. This tends to be more of a problem for men, who have been raised to think of independence as the ultimate virtue and to see asking for help as a sign of weakness. (Picture the average married couple out for a drive in the country and not sure of how to get where they are going. Typically the wife will want to stop and ask directions, while the husband will insist on driving a little farther and trying to find it on his own.) But the assumption of self-sufficiency is becoming a problem for women too, as more women attempt to get ahead in business by emulating men. Is it really a sign of strength and good judgment to refuse help when help is offered? It is a mistake to see religion as the refuge of the insecure and the emotionally dependent, and agnosticism as the domain of the brave and the independent. All people are dependent and vulnerable. Churches are filled with people brave enough to admit that the most important things in their lives are things they cannot get entirely by their own efforts. Their plea to God is not "I'm weak; do this for me," but "I'm only human, be with me as I struggle to become truly human."

A man came to see me some years ago. He had been a middle-management executive for a local electronics company, and had had a nervous breakdown when stress at work and stress at home added up to more than he could handle. He lost his job and spent several months in a hospital psychiatric unit. He was out now, looking for a job and trying to put his life together again. His question to me was "Should I tell prospective employers about my hospitalization, or will they think that I'm mentally unstable and be afraid to hire me?" I told him that he should be truthful about it, both because it was nothing to be ashamed of and because they would likely find out anyway. "If you had been hospitalized with a broken leg, because you had put more strain on your thigh bone than it could bear, would you be embarrassed by it? Don't be embarrassed by your experience. Turn it into a strength; present yourself as a person who has the insight and courage to recognize his problems and get help with them." He did, and his personal and professional lives have gone smoothly since.

In the same way, the person who acknowledges his need for what religion offers is not admitting weakness. He is displaying wisdom. There is an old Yiddish proverb, "Better a sinner who knows he is a sinner than a saint who knows he is a saint." A religious institution does not open its doors only to saints, nor does it promise to turn people into saints when they walk through its doors. Its doors are open to all, but especially to the person who realizes his faults and understands that he needs help to become someone who likes himself better. Just as the person who never goes to the doctor because he is afraid of what he might find out may be sicker than the person who gets regular checkups, the person who dismisses religion as being only for the emotionally needy may be the one who needs it most. He has not learned the very first lesson of religion, that we are all spiritually incomplete people and we all have room to grow.

Sometimes organized religion, the local church or synagogue, turns off the potential seeker because he or she sees it as a gathering of unimpressive, flawed, insecure people. But more often, the seeker is repelled by the smugness of a congregation that sees itself as a gathering of the elite. Like the man who tried to end a religion discussion by saying, "We're never going to convince each other; you go on worshiping God in your way, and I'll go on worshiping Him in His," religiously committed people sometimes cross the boundary between commitment and condescension, between believing in the truth of their religion and dismissing all other religious claims as false. In the minds of many, such fervor is synonymous with fanaticism, the smug insistence that "We are right and on our way to heaven; you are wrong and going to hell if you don't join us." Our image of a religious leader is less likely to be Mother Teresa in Calcutta or the black Baptist preacher trying to offer inner-city youngsters an alternative to drugs and crime. It is more likely to be the Ayatollah Khomeini or the leader of some bizarre cult brainwashing his disciples into letting him control every aspect of their lives. Or it may be the image of a Sunday-morning televangelist with his expensive suit and haircut and his constant appeals for money.

Why does a good thing like religion so easily get distorted into something repulsive like fanaticism, bigotry, or the total surrender of our free will? Why is it, as someone once said, that "we have just enough religion to hate each other but not enough to love each other"? And why is it that these extreme forms of religion are flourishing today?

No one could have predicted the upsurge of fundamentalism that we are witnessing in Protestant and Catholic Christianity, in Judaism, and in Islam. When I was a seminary student thirty years ago, we confidently anticipated that Orthodox Judaism would disappear by the end of the century, as the immigrant generation gave way to a native-born, college-educated American Jewish community. We saw rational religion replacing blind faith, and we championed the right of the enlightened individual to decide for himself what religion would mean to him. We worried about where we would find scribes and ritual slaughterers without Orthodox institutions. Today, Orthodox Judaism is growing in numbers, and in confidence and assertiveness, making inroads especially among the successful and best educated. Similarly, Protestant scholars predicted that as Americans moved from the country to the cities, became better educated, and earned more money, they would leave their rural church affiliations and join one of the more "respectable" mainline denominations. To their astonishment, they have seen people of means and sophistication pass by the mainline churches and affiliate with the fundamentalist church down the street.

Some of the reasons for this are healthy. People are looking for religious seriousness, and are not finding it in the churches and synagogues which have rooted themselves in a philosophy of accommodation to the world around them. If the modern world is part of the problem, with its competitiveness and materialism, why join a church which reflects and celebrates that society, and boasts of its readiness to compromise with the secular world rather than present an alternative to it? When the local Roman Catholic church offers Saturday-afternoon Masses for the convenience of people who like to go skiing or sleep late on Sunday mornings, isn't it saying in effect, "We have lost the battle to make Sunday the Lord's Day; we surrender"? And for everyone who is grateful for the opportunity to attend Mass without giving up skiing and praises the church for its flexibility, isn't there likely to be at least one worshiper who would prefer a church that says, "You have to choose—either God or the secular lifestyle"?

If we are vaguely troubled by the American value system, we will feel let down by a church or synagogue whose message from the pulpit is "Everything is wonderful." We will respond rather to a voice that says, "Everything is not wonderful. Some things are seriously wrong with the way you and your neighbors live." But in the churches of the comfortable and the affluent, we rarely hear that message. Dean Kelley, author of *Why the Fundamentalist Churches Are Growing* (published in 1972), tells of the Methodist minister who learned that the outstanding teenager in his congregation, president of his church youth fellowship, was leaving to join a fundamentalist congregation. Her parting words to him were "if only you believed what you believe as strongly as they believe what they believe."

To some degree, this resurgence of religious orthodoxy may simply reflect a periodic swing of the pendulum. After all, it is happening in Judaism, Christianity, and Islam. It is happening in America, in Europe, and in the Middle East. And it is paralleled by a resurgence of conservative values in politics and a return to "basics" in education. Part of the explanation may be that we are witnessing a reaction to the excessive freedom and the disregard for traditional values we saw in the 1960s, the torrent of violence, profanity, and casual sex. (It is interesting that one of the most popular films about extramarital sex [which used to be known as adultery] in the 1950s was *The Seven Year Itch*. Extramarital temptation was a subject for comedy, and the only moral issue was whether the man's wife would find out. In the 1960s, the corresponding movie was *Bob and Carol and Ted and Alice*. Extramarital sex was now taken seriously; it was no longer funny. But it was good. It increased the total amount of love in the world, and that was what the world needed. By 1987, following the emergence of herpes and AIDS, the reaction had set in, and the big extramarital sex movie was *Fatal Attraction*. Its message: when the genie of uncontrolled lust is let out of the bottle, the results are too horrible to contemplate.)

Faced with a choice between no rules and too many rules, many intelligent people who are not bigots or fanatics may be saying the same thing their predecessors said in the 1960s: "We know where the one leads, and we don't like it. Let's try the other." The difference is that the rebels of the 1960s ended up extremely permissive. Today's rebels become conservatives.

I admire and applaud that aspect of the revival of strict, demanding religion which rejects the vulgarity of the modern world, even as I choose not to be part of it. Remembering Robert Frost's line, "Most of the change we think we see in life is due to truths being in and out of favor," I cherish my liberal religious values and await the day when they will be fashionable again. But at the same time, there is another part of the religious revival that troubles me deeply. Not all of it is a principled rejection of the vulgarity of American society. Some of it is a fear of freedom, a fear of making choices. The world has become too complicated for us. We can't understand it. We don't know whom to trust. So we are

vulnerable to the person who says, "Too many decisions? Let me simplify life for you. Make one decision,
to buy our package, and you will never have to agonize
over choosing between right and wrong again. We will
tell you what is right, and we will surround you with a
supportive, loving community to reassure you that, no
matter what the misguided souls of the outside world
may say, you are on the right path."

At its worst, this vulnerability gives us an Adolf
Hitler, who strode into the moral decay and economic
ruin of Germany in the 1930s and said, "Follow me,
never question me, and I will lead you out of this." In its
more benign form, it gives us people who are shaped by
their religious commitment into rigid, judgmental,
humorless souls. I think of some Orthodox Jews I
know who live their days in constant fear that they have
inadvertently broken one of God's rules, or of the pious
Christians who fear that they may have contaminated
their souls by watching a lingerie ad on television. They
are not the best advertisements for what religious
involvement does for a person.

When I meet someone who is totally committed to the
idea that his way is the right way and that all who differ
from him are wrong, a person who cannot even contemplate the idea that one of his beliefs might be mistaken
("If the whale didn't swallow Jonah, then the whole
Bible is a pack of lies, and murder and adultery are per-
missible"), or a person who feels the need to convert me
to his point of view (I get three or four letters a week
from people like that), I suspect that if I scratched far
enough below the surface of that person, I would find a

vein of fear. I suspect that fear, not faith, not love of God or love of life, is that person's animating emotion — the fear that what he has based his life on may not be true. I suspect the person is afraid that, if intelligent, honorable people reject what he affirms, he may in fact be wrong. The foundation of his entire life may turn out to be built on sand.

Fear is not a very attractive emotion. It rarely brings out the best in us. I think of one congregation I know where a proposed change in liturgy, expanding the role of women in the service, has divided the congregation into two warring camps. Friendships of twenty years' standing have been strained. Arguments escalate into fistfights in the temple. Little children are told what terrible people their parents are for supporting the "wrong" position. Why are people so emotionally involved in a minor matter of theological interpretation? The answer, I believe, is fear, fear that their most cherished beliefs might not be shared by their friends and neighbors. When you need to believe in something, and part of you suspects that it might not be true, you work very hard to quiet that inner voice of doubt, and you can find it very upsetting when someone says out loud what you are trying so hard not to hear. That is why religious disagreements about apparently minor matters can become so intense and so bitter.

"Just enough religion to hate each other"? Does religious fervor have to lead to fanaticism, to a hatred of other, "competing" religions? I would hope (in spite of a great deal of historical evidence, I admit) that, if religious bigotry is born of fear, the fear that what I have staked my life—and sometimes my afterlife—on may be wrong, religion properly understood can lead to serenity, a quiet self-confidence in the validity of my beliefs which will make fear of difference unnecessary. Religion may attract more than its share of frightened, insecure people, but it does not have to leave them frightened and insecure.

Is it possible for me to believe that my faith is true without having to believe that yours is false? Can I accept you in your affirmation of a different faith only if I don't care that deeply about my own? I cherish the words of the Reverend William Sloane Coffin, who said, "We can build a community out of seekers of truth, but not out of possessors of truth," presumably because not all of them would have the same truth, but each of them would feel obliged to defend his truth as being the only valid one.

The scene is an all too familiar one. Debbie had always been one of my favorite young people in the congregation, bright, attractive, enthusiastic about her religious studies and about coming to services. This morning, she is home from college and has come to see me, accompanied by her boyfriend, who is not Jewish. She can't understand why her parents are troubled by the relationship. "I mean, it's not as if Ken were a priest or something. His parents are Protestant but don't even know what kind of Protestant they are. Ken hasn't been in church since he was fifteen. And it's not as if my parents were so pious either. You know as well as anyone, Rabbi, they only come for the High Holy Days. I'm the only one who was ever religious in my family. If it doesn't bother me, why should it bother them?"

Debbie has turned to me because she remembers from her teenage years how involved I have been in interfaith and interracial activities. She expects me to side with her against her parents, and endorse her view that religious differences don't matter. She is hurt and disappointed when I tell her that I too have problems with the prospect of her marrying Ken. "It's not that I believe Jews are better than other people or different from other people. You know I don't believe that. But it saddens me to see two bright young people like yourselves start out in life with the notion that religion will never play any role in your home because the two of you don't share a religion in common. There are so many things that religion could add to a family that you two are ruling out from the start."

At this point, Ken speaks for the first time in the interview. "No offense, Rabbi, but that attitude is exactly what turns a lot of young people off religion. You care a lot more about the institutions, the label, the brand name of whatever religion you practice, than you do about our feelings. We believe we can be honest, ethical people without having to go to a particular church or synagogue building every week."

I answered, "Ken, I don't think that's a fair accusation. I do care about institutions, because I believe people need institutions, not just because I'm employed by one. I don't believe you can practice religion in general any more than you can speak language in general. You have to speak a specific language, and to follow a specific, consistent, coherent religion. But I care about people a lot more than I care about institutions. I'm taking the position I am precisely because I care about Debbie and you. It's easy to say, at age twenty-two or twenty-three, that religious affiliation may be important to your parents but it doesn't mean anything to you. But how do you know you won't be very different people ten years from now? You're certainly different people today than you were ten years ago. Things that don't matter to you now may matter immensely to you ten years down the road. You may develop spiritual needs you can't foresee today, and they will become a source of serious conflict between you. Things may happen to you, good things or bad things, the birth of a child or the death of someone you love. It will call for a religious response, and instead of responding together you will have to ask, 'which religious response, which religious idiom, my parents' or yours?' "

Debbie was close to tears when she and Ken left my office. Her last words to me were "Why do there have to be so many different religions? Why can't there just be one big religion for everybody? Why does religion have to be something that keeps people apart rather than something that brings them together?"

Why *are* there so many separate religions, each claiming to be truer and more valid than the next? If religion were a provable matter, then we could assume that the multiplicity of religions was a temporary situation. With time, we would find out which claims were true and which were in error. Religion would be like chemistry or astronomy. The more we learned, the more we would be able, with some confidence, to discard false ideas and affirm true ones. But the problem is not only that religious statements are unprovable. (How can anyone prove the truth or falsity of the statement that an angel spoke to Mary, or to Mohammed, or to Joseph Smith?) The problem is that religion is not first and foremost a series of teachings about God. Religion is first and foremost the *community* through which you learn to understand the world and grow to be human.

Religion is the bringing together of people to share the important moments of their lives. In most religions, the people, the community, existed first, and the religion grew out of the people's efforts to understand and sanctify the world. (Christianity is the most notable exception to this rule: The idea existed before the community did, and people became Christians by accepting the idea, which is why statements about God are more prominent in Christianity than in most other world religions. It may also explain why most North American Christians will find my definition of religion as community rather than theology puzzling, though I suspect that Latin-American Catholics will feel at home with it.)

Debbie and Ken had trouble understanding this. They thought that because they didn't disagree on any religious beliefs, they had no religious differences. I tried to explain to them that the issue was not what they believed about God, sin, salvation, or even the morality of abortion or eating pork. The issue was in which religious language and through which religious community would they express their religious impulses? And if they did not share a religious language and community, their answer would have to be "None."

Sociologist Robert Bellah explains that the human race is just too vast for us to know who we are by belonging to it. To establish our identity, we have to identify ourselves as part of some subgroup. That identification has to teach us who we are, in part, by teaching us who we are not. I am male, not female. I am American, not European or Asian. I am a Jew, not a gentile. Realizing who I am not helps me to understand who I am. That is why we identify with our local sports teams (living in Boston, I am a Red Sox fan), and why we feel a loss of identity when the franchise is moved to another city. That is also why, if Debbie and Ken do get married and have children without resolving their religious differences, their children will one day ask them, "I know Daddy is Christian and Mommy is Jewish, but what am I?" And Debbie and Ken will do them no favor by telling them, "You're a little bit of both."

There are different religions because we come from different families, from different backgrounds, from different communities. I once heard a Buddhist theologian tell a Christian minister with whom he appeared on a panel, "To say that Christianity is the only way to God is like saying that your wife is the only woman in the world." For me to claim that my wife is the most wonderful woman in the world, or that my mother is the best cook, or that my local basketball team is the best in the country is a statement of loyalty, not of fact. Such statements do not conflict with what *you* may choose to say about your wife, mother, or basketball team. It is at

least in that sense, the sense that religi
statements of loyalty rather than historical ta
or more religions can be true even if they see the w
differently.

Religions can disagree and still each be true because
people's spiritual needs come in different forms. Just as
a doctor may prescribe two different medications for
two people with the same illness, because the people's
bodies are different, some of us may need and respond
to a religion which stresses man's sinfulness and need of
grace, while others may need one which urges them to
pull themselves up by their own bootstraps.

If religious claims to truth were statements of fact,
then when they differed, at most only one of them could
be true. It would be like a mathematical problem to
which there was only one right answer but many wrong
ones. Either God became flesh in the person of Jesus or
He didn't, and there is no middle ground. If your religion is true, then mine must be false. But religious
claims can be true at a level other than the factual one.
Religious claims can be true the way a great novel is
true. It teaches us something valid about the human
condition, even though the characters in the novel
never really existed and the events never took place.
There can be only one right answer to a question like
"What is the biggest state in the United States?" but
there can be many right answers to a question like
"What place in the United States makes you feel proud-
est to be an American when you visit it?"

If believing in the Resurrection makes my Christian
neighbor a better person, more loving and generous,

better able to cope with misfortune and disappointment, then that is a true belief, whether historically true or not. If believing that God commanded him not to eat pork or shellfish gives my Orthodox Jewish friend the gift of controlling his impulses, then his belief is a true belief, irrespective of whether God actually spoke those words. But if either of those beliefs makes these people parochial, narrow-minded, or self-righteous, then their beliefs are religiously false, even if someone could somehow prove that the premise for their beliefs was true.

What keeps people from seeking God, when so many valuable gifts come to those who gain His presence? I think of a man in my congregation who used to attend services with some regularity. One day, he asked if he could see me about a personal problem. He told me he had been stealing money from a family business for which he served as bookkeeper and was ashamed of it. I told him I took his coming to see me as a sign that he wanted to stop, and we spoke of how he might make restitution. Since then, his attendance at synagogue has been infrequent. I once ran into him and asked him about it, and he told me he was embarrassed to come to synagogue because I knew his shameful secret and seeing me reminded him of it.

Sometimes we are distanced from religion because we see it as the voice of our conscience, and that makes us uncomfortable. We don't like to be reminded of our faults. As the writer Maurice Samuel put it, "No man loves his alarm clock."

There is a scene in Bernard Malamud's novel *Dubin's*

Lives in which the hero, a shy, withdrawn professor of literature who has rediscovered his capacity for lust while writing a biography of D. H. Lawrence, succeeds in persuading a young woman whom he has been pursuing to go to a hotel room with him. He feels his efforts at seduction will finally succeed. But as they enter the hotel room, the professor goes to the closet to hang up his coat, and as he does so, he passes a window which overlooks a synagogue where he sees a group of old men at prayer. At that moment, all the fun is drained out of the anticipated assignation.

There will be times when we resent religion for telling us that what we want to do is wrong, even as we sometimes resent our doctor for telling us that our eating or drinking habits are bad for us, or our lawyer for telling us that the brilliant money-making idea we thought up is illegal. For the religious spokesman, the dilemma is acute: How do we give advice without nagging? How do we summon people to rise to a higher, more demanding moral level without coming across as judging them for where they are now (not because where they are now is so praiseworthy but because nagging and condemning are rarely an effective way of changing people)? How do we teach right and wrong without coming across like the Blue Meanies in the Beatles movie *The Yellow Submarine,* dour, life-denying characters whose only pleasure is saying no to everything that sounds like fun?

I believe strongly that one of the primary goals of religion is to teach people to like themselves and feel good about themselves. All my experience has taught

me that people who feel good about themselves will be
more generous, more forgiving of others, less defensive
about their mistakes, more accessible to change, and
better able to cope with misfortune and adversity.
Paradoxically, the person who sees himself or herself as
a good person will be more open to suggestions of
change than the person who is overly conscious of his
or her faults. I am not sure why; it may be that someone
who sees herself as a good person believes in her capacity to become even better, while the unsure person is
likely to say, "What's the point of trying; nothing I do
ever works out the way I want it to." When the voice of
religion is a harsh, judgmental voice that constantly
criticizes us for our faults and keeps telling us how far
we fall short of God's expectations of us, it is less likely
to accomplish what it set out to do. Yet if religion does
not identify our faults and urge us to improve, if it
becomes a cheerleader for the status quo, how will we
ever grow and improve?

I never sit down to write a sermon without summon-
ing up the memory of my family's rabbi when I was a
child in Brooklyn, Rabbi Israel Levinthal. He was a
master preacher and orator. He would never say to us,
"You are doing wrong, you are following the wrong
path; do it differently." Instead he would say, "How
much happier our lives would be if we only incorpo-
rated into them the wisdom of this ancient teaching."
He made us feel that he was giving us a present, the gift
of sage advice, rather than scolding us for not having
thought of it on our own.

When I speak to teenagers in my congregation about

standards of sexual behavior, I understand that I can't simply tell them what I believe, or what my religious tradition teaches, about premarital sex. If I speak only about the wrongness of promiscuity, I made two bad things happen. First, they won't change their behavior because of what I say, because peer pressure and biological urges are stronger. And second, I will be teaching them to think of themselves as nonreligious people because they did not listen to me, and that self-image will only make it harder for me to get through to them the next time. I will end up teaching them either that they are bad people or that religion is irrelevant as a guide. I don't want to come across to them as the grinch who says about everything pleasurable, "Don't, don't." But I certainly don't want to be put in the position of saying, "Go ahead and do what you want," just to keep them listening.

So I try to speak to them in terms of their questions rather than in terms of the religious tradition's answers. I try to start where they are, rather than telling them where I would like them to end up. I don't talk about whether God approves or disapproves of premarital sex. I talk about their own sense of integrity and self-respect and how much they will have lost if they give that away. I talk about the religious principle of taking people's feelings seriously and not exploiting others for our own selfish purposes, any more than we would like them to exploit us. I talk about what makes a person popular, and tell them that my definition of being grown up is not a matter of smoking, drinking, and having sex. Being grown up means being able to control your appetites rather than letting them control you. Being grown up means liking yourself and not depending on other people's approval to feel that you are worthwhile. I do this not as a tactic, a clever way of sneaking my religious message across but because I genuinely believe that what religion offers us all is guidance and not judgment, advice and experience, not condemnation. I worry about preachers and smugly devout people who picture a God who can hardly wait to catch us in a mistake and send us to hell. I could not learn from a teacher if I thought that teacher enjoyed flunking people more than teaching them, to reassure himself that he was stronger and smarter than they were. And I cannot worship a God who set His role as being our judge rather than our teacher.

As in the Hassidic story of the little girl whose hide-and-seek playmates lost interest in finding her, God is absent from our lives because we have stopped looking for Him. Sometimes we have stopped looking because the people who speak on His behalf are small-souled, bigoted, and crass, sometimes because their human flaws and failings are too evident (and perhaps remind us of our own). Sometimes we have stopped looking for God because (like people who keep postponing the visit to the doctor or dentist) we think we know what He will say to us and we don't want to hear it. And sometimes we don't look for God because it never occurs to us that we need Him.

But when, in moments of honest reflection, we are brave enough to confront the emptiness at the very core of our lives, when we are brave enough to ask questions like "Why am I here? How can I manage to do something which has always been too hard for me? How can I learn to like myself better and be less dependent on what others think of me?" we find ourselves wishing we could find our way back to God. But it has been so long that we don't remember the way, and we instinctively mistrust most of the people who loudly volunteer to show us.

How do we find our way back to God? Let us turn one last time to the Book of Psalms, to a little Psalm which I have always liked and which has always said some important things to me. I cherish Psalm 146 because it starts out sounding very abstract and theological, but soon shifts its focus to practical concerns:

Hallelujah! Praise the Lord, O my soul!
I will praise the Lord all my life,
Sing hymns to my God while I exist.
Put not your trust in the great,
In mortal man who cannot save.
His breath departs, he returns to dust;
On that day his plans come to nothing.
Happy is he who has the God of Jacob for his help,
Whose hope is in the Lord his God,
Maker of heaven and earth, the sea and all that is
     therein,
Who keeps faith forever,
Who secures justice for those who are wronged,
Who gives bread to the hungry.
The Lord sets the prisoners free;
The Lord restores sight to the blind;

The Lord makes those who are bent stand straight:
The Lord loves the righteous;
The Lord watches over the stranger,
He gives courage to the orphan and the widow,
But makes the path of the wicked tortuous.
The Lord shall reign forever,
Your God, O Zion, for all generations, Hallelujah.

The Psalm starts out to answer the question, "How do I know there is a God who is greater than any human being, and where can I find Him so that I can praise Him?" But it does not answer that question the way most religious books would. The Psalm does not give any of the traditional proofs of God. Instead, it asks, "Where do you find God?" and answers, "Wherever justice is meted out to the powerless, wherever people share their bread with the hungry, extend freedom to the oppressed, lend a hand to the afflicted, the lonely, and the stranger, God is present." Why else would people be generous, brave, honest, or helpful? Why would people give away their money, contribute their energy and free time, take on the established power structure unless God were at work through them? The believer in God has to answer the question of why there is evil and cruelty in the world. But the atheist has a more difficult challenge. He has to explain why there is love, honesty, generosity, courage, and altruism in the world, and why it feels so good and so right when we let those qualities into our lives.

My friend Rabbi Harold Schulweis of Los Angeles, who is an outstanding, innovative congregational rabbi,

has coined the term "predicate theology." Do you
remember learning in English class that when the verb
of a sentence is a form of the infinitive "to be" *(am, are,
is)*, the part that comes after the verb is not called an
object (since the verb "to be" does not denote action),
but is known as a predicate? "Predicate theology"
means that when we find statements about God that
say, for example, "God is love," "God is truth," "God is
the friend of the poor," we are to concentrate on the
predicate rather than on the subject. Those are not
statements about God; they are statements about love,
truth, and befriending the poor, telling us that those are
divine activities, moments in which God is present.

All those lines in the middle of Psalm 146, telling us
that God "secures justice for those who are wronged,
gives bread to the hungry, sets prisoners free, restores
sight to the blind," are not a description of how God
spends His time. Concentrate on the end of each sentence, rather than on the references to God. Read the
sentences backwards, if you will. Securing justice is a
divine act, a manifestation of God's presence in human
activity. So is feeding the hungry, supporting the poor,
comforting the sick and the lonely. They are not things
that God does; they are things that *we* do, and when we
do them, God is present in our lives. In predicate theology, an atheist is not a person who says, "God has no
meaning for me." He is a person who says, "Helping the
poor and the hungry, working for justice have no meaning for me." If, in our tradition, we believe that God
stands for things like love, courage, and honesty, the
atheist is not the person who denies the existence of

God, but the one who denies the value of love, courage, and honesty.

I once wrote that I found the question "Where is God?" a difficult one to answer. It implies that God is an object, located at a certain point in space, and if we were in the right place (the top of the proper mountain, or in a church or synagogue on the right day at the right hour) we would find God. I suggested that in place of asking "Where is God?" we ask "*When* is God?" Being in God's presence is not a matter of being in the right place but of doing the right things. What has to be happening in our lives for us to feel that we are in the presence of God? Prayer, if we have learned to pray, is one answer, and it can happen anywhere. Love is another. Healing the sick or experiencing the miracle of our own bodies' healing can be an answer. The activities listed in Psalm 146—feeding the hungry, straightening the backs of the oppressed, securing justice for those who have been wronged—are all answers. Religion properly understood is not a series of beliefs about God. It is an inventory of moments in our lives, things we do and things that happen to us, in which the person whose eyes are open will be able to see God.

What sort of world would it be if there were no God? Some people would say it would be a world very much like the one we now have, a world of war and threats of war, of crime and corruption and random cruelty. For me, the answer is even more dismaying. Without God, it would be a world where no one was outraged by crime or cruelty, and no one was inspired to put an end to them. It would be a world where, if we were the victims of crime or misfortune, we would curse our bad luck, and if someone near us was a victim, we would merely feel relief that it happened to her and not to us. But we would have no reason to feel "this is not the way the world is supposed to work," nor would we have any reason to believe that, with enough time and effort, we could make it better.

In a world without God, there would be no more inspiring goal for our lives than self-interest, amassing as many of the good things of life as we could grab. There would be neither room nor reason for tenderness, generosity, helpfulness. We might want to learn, to help us get ahead, but we would have no reason to teach, and whom would we find to teach us?

A world without God would be a flat, monochromatic world, a world without color or texture, a world in which all days would be the same. Marriage would be a matter of biology, not fidelity. Old age would be seen as a time of weakness, not of wisdom. In a world like that, we would cast about desperately for any sort of diversion, for any distraction from the emptiness of our lives, because we would never have learned the magic of making some days and some hours special.

A world without God would be a world in which gravity pulled us down and there was no counterforce to lift us up, to cleanse us if we had sullied ourselves when we stumbled and fell, and assure us that we were worthy of a second chance.

And worst of all, in a world without God, we would be all alone—no one to help us when we had to do something hard, no one to forgive us when we had disappointed ourselves, no one to replenish us when we had come to the point of using ourselves up, and no one to promise us that, even when it was over, it will not be over.

An ancient Greek myth tells of two brothers, Prometheus and Atlas, who offended the gods and were punished. Prometheus was chained to a rock and every day an eagle came and pecked at his defenseless body. Atlas was condemned to carry the weight of the entire world on his shoulders. That was as harsh a punishment as the ancient Greek mind could conjure up. Today, it seems, we have volunteered to play the role of Atlas. We have not offended God, we have dismissed Him, told Him we were grown up enough not to need His help anymore, and offered to carry the weight of the entire world on our shoulders. The question is, when it gets too heavy for us, when there are questions too hard for human knowledge to answer and problems that take more time to solve than any of us have, will we be too proud to admit that we have made a mistake in wanting to carry this world alone? Will we be able to ask for help?

In his classic novel *One Hundred Years of Solitude*, Colombian author Gabriel García Márquez tells of a village where people were afflicted with a strange plague of forgetfulness, a kind of contagious amnesia. Starting with the oldest inhabitants and working its way through the population, the plague causes people to forget the names of even the most common everyday objects. One young man, still unaffected, tries to limit the damage by putting labels on everything. "This is a table," "This is a window," "This is a cow; it has to be milked every morning." And at the entrance to the town, on the main road, he puts up two large signs. One reads "The name of our village is Macondo," and the larger one reads "God exists."

The message I get from that story is that we can, and probably will, forget most of what we have learned in life—the math, the history, the chemical formulas, the address and phone number of the first house we lived in when we got married—and all that forgetting will do us no harm. But if we forget whom we belong to, and if we forget that there is a God, something profoundly human in us will have been lost.

Do you remember the story we told several chapters ago, about how man persuaded God to change places with him for one second, and in that instant refused to give God back His place, so that ever since then, man has replaced God on the divine throne? I find that a frightening story on two counts. First, human beings without God are capable of such terrible cruelty and selfishness. As one of the Karamazov brothers says in Dostoevsky's novel, "If there is no God, everything is permitted." But even worse, human beings without God are so terribly alone in a big, cold, purposeless, unhallowed world.

The bad news is that it is hard to grow a soul when you have lost the knack. Just as it is harder to start a car on a cold morning than it is to keep it running, it is harder to regain a sense of religion, of sacred community, of being in God's presence, once we have lost it. Nurturing a soul is a slow, painstaking process. And it becomes harder still when society offers us so few role models who have done it successfully, and so many diversions to distract us from the effort.

But the good news is that, no matter how hard we may find it to grow a soul, we will not be alone in the striving, "for Thou art with me." Who needs God in a world that could be so beautiful and so holy, in a life that could be so full of meaning and satisfaction, if we only opened our eyes and knew where to look? Who needs God?

I know I do.

I know we do.